The Book of Jonah

The Book of Jonah

An Exegetical Commentary on the Hebrew Text

JOHAN FERREIRA

WIPF & STOCK · Eugene, Oregon

THE BOOK OF JONAH
An Exegetical Commentary on the Hebrew Text

Copyright © 2025 Johan Ferreira. All rights reserved. Except for brief quotations in critical publications or reviews, no part of this book may be reproduced in any manner without prior written permission from the publisher. Write: Permissions, Wipf and Stock Publishers, 199 W. 8th Ave., Suite 3, Eugene, OR 97401.

Wipf & Stock
An Imprint of Wipf and Stock Publishers
199 W. 8th Ave., Suite 3
Eugene, OR 97401

www.wipfandstock.com

PAPERBACK ISBN: 979-8-3852-3882-8
HARDCOVER ISBN: 979-8-3852-3883-5
EBOOK ISBN: 979-8-3852-3884-2

VERSION NUMBER 03/14/25

"Dr. Ferreira's commentary is useful and helpful to understand the book of Jonah, especially for pastors and students who have had a course in Hebrew and who would like to study the original text in depth. The commentary not only offers sound exegesis, but with its methodology and approach, it also serves as a guide to do the exegetical task, a very special feature of the book. It contributes to enriching our learning tools. I welcome its publication and recommend its wide circulation."

WILSON W. CHOW
President Emeritus
China Graduate School of Theology

"As Johan Ferreira notes, when you have got your mind round basic Hebrew, Jonah is an ideal Old Testament book to study. And this commentary is ideal as a companion for studying it. It is a marvellously thorough word-by-word analysis of the text that will enable you to make huge progress in your grasp of Hebrew and in your interaction with the intriguing, engaging, challenging book of Jonah."

JOHN GOLDINGAY
David Allan Hubbard Professor Emeritus of Old Testament
Fuller Theological Seminary

"We welcome the publication of Johan Ferreira's commentary on the book of Jonah. This exegetical commentary on the Hebrew text will enable students and pastors to do proper exegesis of the text and appreciate the beauty of the descriptive narrative in Jonah. The exegetical notes are carefully done and very readable. The introduction gives a good analysis of the themes and purpose of the book. Indeed, it is God who speaks through the book of Jonah, revealing His lovingkindness!"

Joseph Shao
4th General Secretary, Asia Theological Association
President Emeritus
Biblical Seminary of the Philippines

"This all-in-one guide to exegeting the book of Jonah is perfectly suited to students who have completed introductory study of Biblical Hebrew grammar and are ready to undertake exegesis. For each verse, Ferreira presents the Hebrew text, a fluid translation, and concise identification of every grammatical element. Best of all, he offers expert exegetical observations that show the student how the pieces of the text fit together, complemented by relevant historical, geographical, and archaeological information. Exemplifying attention to detail as well as a rich view of the whole, this excellent guide will both form and inform the student."

Daniel Timmer
Professor of Biblical Studies
Puritan Reformed Theological Seminary

Contents

List of Abbreviations | vii

Introduction | 1
1   Jonah Flees | 13
2   Jonah Prays | 60
3   Jonah Preaches | 88
4   Jonah Complains | 116

Selected Bibliography | 145

List of Abbreviations

BOOKS OF THE BIBLE

Old Testament

Gen, Exod, Lev, Num, Deut, Josh, Judg, Ruth, 1–2 Sam, 1–2 Kgs, 1–2 Chr, Ezra, Neh, Esth, Job, Ps, Prov, Eccl, Song, Isa, Jer, Lam, Ezek, Dan, Hos, Joel, Amos, Obad, Jonah, Mic, Nah, Hab, Zeph, Hag, Zech, Mal

New Testament

Matt, Mark, Luke, John, Acts, Rom, 1–2 Cor, Gal, Eph, Phil, Col, 1–2 Thess, 1–2 Tim, Titus, Phlm, Heb, Jas, 1–2 Pet, 1–2–3 John, Jude, Rev

BIBLE VERSIONS

ASV	American Standard Version
CSB	Christian Standard Bible
ESV	English Standard Version
GB	Geneva Bible
GNT	Good News Translation
NASB	New American Standard Bible
NET Bible	New English Translation Bible

List of Abbreviations

NIV	New International Version
NKJV	New King James Version
NLT	New Living Translation
NRSV	New Revised Standard Version
YLT	Young's Literal Translation

Introduction

ALTHOUGH ANYONE MAY READ this short commentary with profit, it is especially geared towards students of Biblical Hebrew. After one has completed foundational units in Hebrew vocabulary, grammar, and syntax, one needs to develop skills for exegesis.[1] Many students of theology spend considerable time in procuring the elements of Biblical Hebrew; however most students do not continue to use Hebrew later on in ministry. It is often unfortunate that the outlay of time and effort during the early years of theological study does not return dividends, but it is especially regrettable that the rich treasures contained in the Scriptures continue to lie buried in the original text for those who rely only on translations.

There are many reasons for this negligence. Life is busy, and ministry is beset with distractions. But a major reason why most students and preachers do not consult the Hebrew text in sermon preparation is because they have not mastered the skills for Hebrew exegesis or have not been taught how to make use of Hebrew in studying the Bible. The usage of an instrument (or skill) is directly proportional to the practical benefits received. Therefore, this commentary aims to provide further training in original language exegesis by illustrating the significance of Hebrew for

---

1. In order to utilize Biblical Hebrew well, students need to master three elements. Firstly, students need to be familiar with the working vocabulary of Biblical Hebrew (around five hundred words). Secondly, students need to have a good understanding of Hebrew grammar and syntax. Then, thirdly, and most importantly, students must master the skills of interpreting Hebrew for exegesis.

understanding and teaching the book of Jonah. It intends to fill the gap between learning the basics of Hebrew grammar and using Hebrew in practical preparation for teaching and preaching.

The book of Jonah will serve our purposes well. Apart from being an important part of Scripture, which is profitable "for teaching, rebuking, correcting, and training in righteousness" (2 Tim 3:16), it contains superb examples of Hebrew prose and poetry, without being overly long. The four chapters can be studied with much profit. The pertinent terminological, grammatical, and syntactical features of the Hebrew text provide students with many examples of how Hebrew informs our understanding and interpretation of the text. The commentary aims to teach by modeling. After readers have observed how the Hebrew text informs interpretation, the same methods and principles may then be applied to other sections of the Hebrew Bible. Therefore, we would encourage the reader not just to read this commentary for information but to study its methodology carefully, noting how the knowledge of Hebrew is applied for exegetical benefit.

THE TEXT OF THE BOOK OF JONAH

Since we will be working with the original Hebrew text, a few comments on the source text of the book of Jonah may be in order. The Hebrew text of the book of Jonah is remarkably well-preserved. For example, the consonantal text of the major Masoretic manuscripts (e.g., Aleppo Codex, Leningrad Codex, the Snaith Edition, and the Rabbinic Bible) is unerringly the same.[2] Most modern translations use the Leningrad Codex as their base text for the translation of the Old Testament. This text is reproduced in the *Biblia Hebraica Stuttgartensia* (BHS), which is the most widely used critical edition

---

2. Originally, Hebrew script did not contain vowels, nor accents or cantillation marks. The term "Masoretic" stems from "masora," which means "tradition." It is used to describe a group of Jewish textual scholars who preserved and edited the Hebrew Bible during the Middle Ages. Variations among the Masoretic texts mostly pertain to the pointing of vowels and cantillation marks rather than differences within the Hebrew consonantal text.

Introduction

of the Hebrew Bible.[3] Dating from the eleventh century AD, the Leningrad Codex is believed to be "the oldest dated manuscript of the complete Hebrew Bible which has come down to us."[4] According to its editorial note, the codex was completed in AD 1008 in Cairo by Aaron ben Moses ben Asher. The codex is now kept in the National Library of Russia, located in Saint Petersburg.[5]

Apart from the Leningrad Codex, there are many other important texts. The Snaith Edition, based on a manuscript in the British Museum (Or 2626-28), was first published in 1958 by the British and Foreign Bible Society in London. The manuscript was produced in 1483 in Lisbon and was acquired by the British Museum in 1882. It is a typical Masoretic manuscript in the Ben Asher tradition. Another important codex is the Aleppo Codex, which is according to some scholars a more accurate witness to the Masoretic text. It is earlier than the Leningrad Codex, dating to around AD 930. However, most of the Pentateuch has been lost during anti-Jewish disturbances in Aleppo in 1947.[6] The Rabbinic Bible was published by Daniel Bomberg in Venice in two editions in 1517-18 and in 1525 under the editorship of Felix Pratensis and Jacob Ben Chayyim.[7] This Hebrew text was published together with Targum Onkelos and several traditional Jewish commentaries. It is probably one of the most remarkable achievements in the early history of the printing press due to the detailed amount of

---

3. The successor to the BHS, the *Biblia Hebraica Quinta* (BHQ), has now been completed in seven volumes. It also uses the Leningrad Codex as its base text but provides a new textual apparatus with notes evaluating the strength of significant variants.

4. Kahle, *Cairo Geniza*, 132; cf. Kittel, *Biblia Hebraica Stuttgartensia*, xii. Most Old Testament books circulated independently or in smaller collections before the current era.

5. With the city's name change, perhaps it is time to change the name of the codex to St. Petersburg Codex.

6. The Hebrew University Bible Project (HUBP) employed the Aleppo Codex as its base text. The Jewish synagogue in Damascus also preserved another manuscript based on the Aleppo Codex, which also dates to the tenth century (National Library of Israel, ms. Heb 5702).

7. The second edition is also known as the Mikraot Gedolot (meaning "Great Scriptures").

typesetting required for the publication. Until the publication of the Leningrad Codex, most translations in the West, including the King James Version of 1611, utilized this text for the source text of the Old Testament.

Another ancient manuscript in the Masoretic tradition, which contains the Former and Latter Prophets, is housed in the Karaite synagogue in Cairo; it is referred to as the Cairo Codex (or Codex Cairensis). According to its colophon, the manuscript was completed in the year AD 895, but recent research dates it to the eleventh century. With respect to the Masoretic manuscripts, we may likewise mention the Codex Sassoon, which was recently sold at an auction for $38.1 million. Based on carbon dating, it appears to stem from the ninth or tenth century. However, the first ten chapters of Genesis are missing from the codex. It is also significant to note that much of the book of Jonah (1:1–16; 2:1, 3–10; 3:1–3; 4:4–11) has been preserved in three fragments from the Dead Sea Scrolls (4Q76, 4Q81, 4Q82). These witnesses, dating to the first century AD, are around a thousand years earlier than the Leningrad Codex and correspond by and large to the Masoretic text. There are no important textual variations.

Finally, we may refer to the Septuagint (abbreviated as LXX). The Septuagint describes a collection of manuscripts, mostly dating from the third to fifth centuries AD, which provides a Greek translation of the Hebrew Old Testament. According to Jewish tradition, the Pentateuch was translated into Greek in Alexandria, Egypt, in the third century BC. Scholars have confirmed this early origin and provenance of the Greek translation of the Pentateuch. However, the rest of the Hebrew Old Testament was probably translated in Israel during the second century BC. The entire Greek text of the book of Jonah is contained in Codex Vaticanus (AD 325–50) and Codex Sinaiticus (AD 330–350). Other early Greek manuscripts of the Old Testament have also been discovered. One significant Greek manuscript of the minor prophets which dates to around 50 BC to AD 50 was discovered at Nahal Hever, a cave near Engedi. It is designated as 8ḤevXII and contains the

Introduction

following sections: Jonah 1:14–16; 2:1–7; 3:2–5, 7–10; and 4:1–2, 5.[8] Another ancient Greek scroll, which dates to the Bar Kochba revolt (c. AD 132), was discovered in a cave at Wadi Murabbaʾat. It is designated as MurXII and preserves the text of the whole book of Jonah. According to the eminent textual critic, Emmanuel Tov, the Masoretic text and the Septuagint reflect the same textual tradition in the book of Jonah.[9] We will refer to a few interesting textual variants from the LXX in the commentary.

OUTLINE, THEME, AND PURPOSE

The book of Jonah is one of the most well-known stories ever told. It does not cease to fascinate children and to challenge scholars alike. In terms of its literary form, imagery, and meaning, the book is both simple and profound. Moreover, the book of Jonah is unique among the prophetical books. It is not about the message of the prophet but rather about the prophet himself. And, unlike the other biblical prophets, Jonah was disobedient to the call of the Lord. Yet, ultimately, the Lord still achieved his purposes for Nineveh through his prophet Jonah.

Reading the book of Jonah should not be isolated from its context within the canon of Scripture. No independent copies of the book of Jonah have been preserved, and as far as we can tell the book always circulated and was always read as part of the Hebrew Bible. Certainly, the Hebrew Bible provides the main source for the author's theological perspective, vocabulary, and spirituality. Therefore, we should also read the book of Jonah within the covenantal or salvation historical framework of the Bible. The book is not an independent story but is part of the history of redemption which finds fulfilment in the Lord Jesus Christ. The central meaning of the book extends beyond the relationship between the Jews and the gentiles but foreshadows the ministry of Christ. Since this commentary focuses on the significance of the Hebrew text for

---

8. The manuscript is now housed in the Rockefeller Museum in Jerusalem.

9. Tov, "Textual Value of the Septuagint Version of the Minor Prophets," 129–47.

exegesis, we will refrain from discussing the message of the book in much depth in the commentary.

Understanding the basic outline, major theme, and intended purpose of a literary work is crucial for interpreting the details of the narrative. In general, ancient authors did not write arbitrarily but were erudite writers who constructed their texts according to definite goals. This sophistication certainly applies to biblical literature. Therefore, from the perspective of the teacher and preacher, grasping the overarching theme and purpose of a book is crucial for clearly communicating the details of its content. Since every passage or literary unit relates directly to the overall theme and purpose of the book, we must constantly recall the book's overarching theme and purpose. Details of the text must be interpreted in light of the book's principal concerns. The application of the text to our current context must also be consistent with the main purpose of the original author or editors. Therefore, understanding the outline, theme, and purpose of a book will give us confidence, clarity, and a useful framework in which to communicate the prophetic message to hearers today.

Many commentators naturally divide the book of Jonah into four sections or scenes, corresponding to the four chapter divisions.[10] These divisions are variously titled but they more or less indicate the same meaning: 1) Jonah Flees (1:1–17); 2) Jonah Prays (2:1–10); 3) Jonah Preaches (3:1–10); and 4) Jonah Complains (4:1–11).[11] Some authors prefer a simpler two-section division:

---

10. The four-chapter divisions were inserted into the text by Stephen Langton, the Archbishop of Canterbury, in 1227. Rabbi Nathan added verse divisions to the Old Testament in 1448, and Robert Estienne similarly added verse divisions to the New Testament in 1555. The Geneva Bible, published in 1560, was the first English Bible to insert both chapter and verse divisions. Consequently, most subsequent translations of the Bible have followed this practice. There are no chapter divisions in Codex Sinaiticus. Paragraph divisions are indicated in Codex Vaticanus at the chapter divisions by means of the outdentation of the line. In the Hebrew Codex Sassoon and Leningrad Codex there is a chapter division (an empty line before chapter 3), but there are no divisions between chapters 1 and 2 and chapters 3 and 4.

11. See Perowne, *Obadiah and Jonah*, 3; and Manley et al., *New Bible Handbook*, 248.

Introduction

1) Jonah's First Commission or the Prophet at Sea (1:1—2:10); and 2) Jonah's Second Commission or the Prophet at Nineveh (3:1—4:11).[12] A somewhat more complex analysis is to divide the book into seven scenes: 1) Jonah's Call (1:1–3); 2) The Storm (1:4–16); 3) The Great Fish (1:17—2:10); 4) The Second Call (3:1–3a); 5) Preaching in Nineveh (3:3b–10); 6) Jonah's Prayer (4:1–3); and 7) The Lord's Questions (4:4–11).[13]

Unravelling the theme of the book of Jonah requires more careful deliberation. From the narrative plot we may observe that God goes to great lengths to save Nineveh from disaster. Even though God's prophet is disobedient, God causes a storm endangering the lives of others, prepares a fish to preserve Jonah, and then commissions him a second time to go to Nineveh. However, the story does not conclude with the extraordinary conversion of the Ninevites. More remarkable is Jonah's anger about God relenting concerning judgment. And so, the story has no denouement but concludes with a question: "And should I not pity Nineveh?" In other words, the intention of the story is much more than just God's desire to spare the Ninevites; it is about the attitude of Israel towards God's attributes and actions. God wants the Ninevites, and especially Jonah, to know who he is—what he does and what he requires—and then to have similar sentiments.

The plot of the book is self-evident. God calls Jonah, although he is far away in Israel, to go to Nineveh and preach against it. Obviously, the intention behind Jonah's mission is so that the Ninevites may repent from evil and be saved from God's judgment. Jonah, however, disobeys and sails off in the opposite direction. Yet, God causes a great storm so that the boat is unable to reach its intended destination. Through the storm and the casting of lots,

---

12. See Patterson and Hill, *Cornerstone Biblical Commentary*, 248–51; Wiseman, Baker, Alexander, and Waltke, *Obadiah, Jonah and Micah*, 105. According to *The NIV Study Bible*, 1) Jonah Flees His Mission (chapters 1–2); 2) Jonah Reluctantly Fulfills His Mission (chapters 3–4) (1364–65). According to *The Reformation Study Bible* (Sproul, 1564), 1) Jonah, Disobedient and Delivered (chapters 1–2); 2) Jonah, Obedient and Rebuked (chapters 3–4). Also see Trible, *Rhetorical Criticism*, 109–17.

13. See Limburg, *Jonah*, 28.

the sailors believe that the storm has come upon them on account of Jonah. In order to calm the storm and avert danger, with Jonah's recommendation, they cast the disobedient prophet into the sea. Then, again, God intervenes by preparing a fish to swallow Jonah. After Jonah's prayer for deliverance, God commands the fish to vomit Jonah out onto dry land. The call of the Lord then comes a second time to Jonah, urging him to go to Nineveh. This time Jonah obeys and goes to Nineveh. Astonishingly, the people of Nineveh repent from their evil ways and pray for compassion. Consequently, the Lord does not send calamity, and the city is preserved. However, the story does not finish there. Jonah is dissatisfied with the outcome of his mission and complains to God, even desiring death rather than accepting the situation. God then engages with his prophet through the object lesson of the short-lived bush to change Jonah's attitude with respect to the Ninevites and especially with respect to God. The key verse that reflects this theme and unlocks the subtleties of the narrative plot is Jonah's objection in chapter 4 verse 2: "You are a gracious and compassionate God, slow to anger and abundant in lovingkindness, and one who relents concerning calamity" (NASB). Therefore, we may suggest the following theme for the book of Jonah: God intervenes in nature and history to save Nineveh as well as engages verbally with his prophet Jonah so that he may be affected by God's grace and so sympathize with the predicament of others. The book demonstrates, despite Jonah's disobedience, how the Lord, being abundant in mercy, goes to great lengths to save Nineveh. But the Lord not only saves Nineveh, he also continues to interact with his recalcitrant prophet to transform his mind and heart to reflect God's own concern for the lost.

The theme of the book is intricately related to its purpose, which is to foster genuine engagement and relationship with God. For the author, it is not simply a matter of repenting and obeying God's will; it is about knowing God and developing the same "heart" as God. The Ninevites should know that God is holy and righteous; he will by no means overlook evil but desires that people live righteously. So too, Jonah should not just know that

Introduction

God is merciful and gracious but should also delight in and be moved by God's mercy and grace. This is also God's intention for New Testament Christians: for them to be affected by the love and grace of the Lord Jesus so that they may also be transformed to reflect his glory and grace.

The ultimate purpose of the book, as with all good literature, is directed towards the reader. By the time the reader is reading the book, Jonah had passed on to receive his reward long ago. It no longer matters how Jonah responded; what matters now is how the reader or the listener responds. The main protagonist of the story is God. Jonah serves as the antagonist. The sailors, the fish, and the Ninevites serve as minor characters in the story. The main plot does not relate to the unbelief of the gentiles or to the relationship between Israel and the gentiles but to the tension between God and his prophet Jonah. In a comparable way, the book of Jonah addresses the reader or the listener. Through his word, actions, and patience, God wants to change the audience's mind and heart regarding the gentiles and then especially regarding God himself. God's people are called to be his witnesses, but they will only be adequate witnesses when their attitude and behavior reflect God's heart of abundant loving-kindness. In short, the purpose of the book is for God's people to have God's heart (Jer 9:23-24).

HEBREW POETRY

Since chapter 2 of the book of Jonah largely consists of a poem or a psalm, it is appropriate to introduce some of the salient features of Hebrew poetry to the reader. From a literary perspective, there are significant differences between prose and poetry. Hebrew prose is carried along by the verb, action is predominant and there is little introspection by the characters in the narrative. The main characteristics of Hebrew poetry consist of parallelism, rhythm, versification, rich imagery, and introspection. Ancient Hebrew poetry shared these characteristics with many of its surrounding literatures.

The Book of Jonah

Parallelism, first described by Robert Lowth, consists of a certain kind of correspondence between adjacent lines.[14] It is a way of repeating, which helps to show what the point of the author is. It can be either semantic or grammatical parallelism (or both). Three basic kinds have been recognized: 1) synonymous parallelism (two similar lines/ideas); 2) antithetic parallelism (two opposite lines/ideas), and 3) synthetic parallelism (one line/idea is expanded or completed by the second line/idea).[15] Professor of the Hebrew Bible James Kugel has amplified our understanding of synonymous parallelism.[16] According to Kugel, strictly speaking there is no such thing as synonymous parallelism (i.e., two lines with exactly the same meaning). The second line always adds something to the first. The second line continues to tell a story and carries the meaning forward or intensifies the meaning (i.e., A *and what is more* B). Kugel's insight is significant for understanding biblical poetry.

Rhythm refers to the stress pattern of the lines, indicated by the accents. Several standard stress patterns have been identified (e.g., 2+2, 3+3, 3+2 sequences), but it should be observed that Hebrew rhythm is not regular (many scholars deny the presence of meter within Hebrew poetry). Of course, Hebrew rhythm can only be studied in the original Hebrew text.

The most basic element of a Hebrew poem is the colon, which refers to a single clause. A line is usually made up of two cola, referred to as a bi-colon, and a line is sometimes made up of a tri-colon. Two lines may then form a couplet. A stanza (or verse) is the combination of several lines into one sense unit or a unit of meaning. All the stanzas together make up the poem (or psalm).

As is common in all poetry, Hebrew poetry uses a number of literary devices, such as simile (use of "as" or "like"), metaphor, irony, symbolism, chiasm, acrostics, alliteration, allusion, anaphora

---

14. See Lowth, *Lectures on the Sacred Poetry of the Hebrews*.

15. Some scholars have identified up to eight distinct kinds of parallelism, which, in addition to the three common types mentioned above, include climactic parallelism, emblematic parallelism, alternate parallelism, and chiastic parallelism. See Watson, *Classical Hebrew Poetry*, and Petersen and Richards, *Interpreting Hebrew Poetry*.

16. See Kugel, *Idea of Biblical Poetry*.

Introduction

(repetition of a word at the beginning of several verses), imagery, onomatopoeia, personification, reification (to treat an abstraction as if it had concrete existence), double meaning, paronomasia, etc.

As over against prose narrative, the use of the article and the relative pronoun is rare in poetry, whereas the use of tenses is much more flexible. With respect to content, poetry contains much more reflection and expression of feelings than prose, which is more matter of fact. When readers study chapter 2 of the book of Jonah they may return to this section and note the differences between prose and poetry in the Hebrew Bible.

A NOTE ON THE FORMAT OF THE COMMENTARY

The commentary provides a verse-by-verse analysis of the book of Jonah under three headings. Firstly, the section *Hebrew Text and Translation* presents the original text from the Leningrad Codex followed by an English translation. Since the commentary focuses on the Hebrew text, the English translation tends to follow a word-for-word or formal equivalence approach to the text. Words or phrases in italics do not appear in the Hebrew text but have been supplied to complete the English syntax. It would be beneficial for students to use a good modern translation (such as the NKJV, ESV, or NASB) alongside this commentary. Also note that the commentary follows the versification of the Hebrew text, which is different from the English versions at the end of chapter 1 and in chapter 2. The English translation will follow the tradition of translating the tetragrammaton (the divine name "Yahweh") with the capitalized "LORD" (written in small capitals).[17] Secondly, the *Grammatical Analysis* lists and analyses every Hebrew word in terms of grammar or syntactic function. The general or dictionary meaning of the word is provided in brackets or inverted commas. It will be

---

17. This convention stems from the Septuagint which translates the Hebrew divine name יהוה ("Yahweh") with the Greek word κύριος, meaning "Lord." The Latin translations followed the cue from the Septuagint and used the term *Dominus* for the divine name, which also means "Lord." This tradition set the stage for most European translations.

good if Hebrew students attempt their own translation and parsing of the textual elements before consulting the guide. The commentary employs traditional nomenclature to refer to the Hebrew stems or verbal forms (e.g., Qal, Nifal, Piel, Pual, Hifil, Hithpael). Finally, the *Exegetical Notes* constitute the bulk of the commentary. The notes are intended as a resource for students to develop their own exegetical skills in using Hebrew for interpretation, teaching, and preaching. Since the commentary is primarily intended as an aid to those with a basic knowledge of Hebrew to improve their use of Hebrew for exegesis, it will not provide a comprehensive commentary on matters regarding historical background, theology, spirituality, and contemporary application of the text. Readers are encouraged to consult the standard commentaries on the book of Jonah, which focus on theological interpretation.[18] Through studying the exegetical notes, the reader will notice that the difference in reading from a translation and the Hebrew text is substantial. Although reading from a good translation should enable the reader to grasp the key points of the text, in terms of the full meaning, assurance of understanding and color, the knowledge one gains from reading the Hebrew text is significantly richer than from reading a translation.

---

18. For example, see the commentaries by Wolff, *Obadiah and Jonah*; Sasson, *Jonah*; and Nogalski, *Reading and Hearing the Book of the Twelve*. Ralph Martin, *Commentary on Jonah*, is excellent in terms of theological insight and personal application, and Daniel Timmer, *Gracious and Compassionate God*, may also be studied with much profit.

1

Jonah Flees

VERSE 1

Hebrew Text and Translation:

וַיְהִי֙ דְּבַר־יְהוָ֔ה אֶל־יוֹנָ֥ה בֶן־אֲמִתַּ֖י לֵאמֹֽר׃

And it came to pass that the word of the LORD came to Jonah, the son of Amittai, saying,

Grammatical Analysis:

וַיְהִי	Qal, imperfect *waw*-consecutive, third-person, masculine, singular (הָיָה, to be, become, is)
דְּבַר	noun, masculine, singular, construct form (דָּבָר, word, matter, thing)
יְהוָה	proper name, "Yahweh," or conventionally "the LORD"
אֶל	preposition ("to" or "towards")
יוֹנָה	proper name, "Jonah" (alternative meaning, "dove")
בֶן	noun, masculine, singular, construct form (בֵּן, son)

The Book of Jonah

אֲמִתַּי   proper name, "Amittai" (from אֱמֶת, truth, faithfulness)

לֵאמֹר   Qal, infinitive, construct (אָמַר, to say), with preposition לְ (to)

Exegetical Notes:

1. The imperfect *waw*-consecutive וַיְהִי (apocopated form) provides one of the keys to the interpretation of the book of Jonah. It is the normal way of beginning a historical narrative.[1] This stylistic cue communicates to the reader that the author is writing history. References to "Jonah, the son of Amittai," an eighth century prophet (2 Kgs 14:25), and the locations of Nineveh, Joppa, and Tarshish further underscore the historicity of the book. There is no doubt that the author considered the contents of the book to be historical events and wants the reader to understand the message of the book within a historical framework. This is the first interpretative key that the book provides to the hearer; it is explicit in the Hebrew text.

2. The imperfect *waw*-consecutive assumes a preceding history or event since historical narrative theoretically begins with the perfect followed by the imperfect *waw*-consecutive.[2] Wolff links it to the book of Obadiah, however, apart from the canonical order, there is nothing to support the suggestion.[3] We may simply link the *waw*-consecutive to the history of Israel as narrated in the Hebrew Bible. In other words, the story of Jonah must be read within the context of the Old Testament Canon. This is the second interpretative key that the reader may deduce from the first word of the text.

---

    1. Eight books in the Old Testament begin in this way (Joshua, Judges, Ruth, 1 and 2 Samuel, Esther, Nehemiah, and Ezekiel).

    2. Ferreira, *Old Testament Hebrew*, 50–51.

    3. Since Obadiah has been connected with the servant of King Ahab who lived before Jonah (1 Kgs 18:1–16), it has been suggested that the book of Obadiah was placed before the book of Jonah in the canonical order.

3. Jonah, identified as a true prophet in 2 Kgs 14:23–25, was the last prophet of the Northern Kingdom. He was a prophet who brought a message of expansion for Israel and one of judgment upon Israel's enemies. He lived in Gath-Hepher, a border region twenty-five kilometers west of the Sea of Galilee.[4] Jonah most probably would have had contact with gentiles during his life in Galilee.

4. The name Jonah means "dove." It is interesting to note that in Hebrew culture a dove was considered to be silly, much as Westerners regard a donkey as a dumb animal or as Chinese consider a pig not to have much sense. In Hos 7:11, Israel is compared to a dove, "being silly and without sense, they call upon Egypt and go to Assyria." Such an absurdity is also evident in the story of Jonah; Jonah was called to go to Nineveh, but he tried to flee to Tarshish, implying (to the reader) that he could thereby escape the presence of the Lord.

5. The construct chain דְּבַר־יְהוָה supplies the subject of the sentence. Although it is anarthrous, the genitive construction makes the expression definite; it is the word of the LORD, not just any word.

6. This phrase דְּבַר־יְהוָה occurs throughout the prophets, but it is significant to note that it first appears in Genesis chapter 15 verse 1 and verse 4 within the context of salvation history. Abraham and Sarah are in the promised land, but they are still childless. God appears to Abraham and assures him through his word that one from his own body will be his heir. In other words, the content of God's word to Abraham (דְּבַר־יְהוָה) is about the covenant promise regarding a son, which functions as a type of Christ. Therefore, the phrase "the word of the LORD" relates to the promise of a Son through whom God's covenantal promises are going to be fulfilled. Abraham believed it. And sure enough, the Bible says, "The LORD counted it to him as righteousness" (Gen

---

4. The Pharisees were obviously wrong when they said that no prophet had arisen from Galilee (cf. John 7:52).

The Book of Jonah

15:6). Within the opening sentence of the book of Jonah there is already a hint to the future fulfilment of the typology of Jonah in the Lord Jesus Christ.

7. The prepositional phrase אֶל־יוֹנָה בֶן־אֲמִתַּי indicates the recipient of the message.

8. The construct chain, "son of Amittai," is also definite and stands in apposition to "Jonah." The name Amittai stems from the Hebrew root אמת which means faithfulness. It appears that Jonah came from an upright and prominent family in Galilee, which makes his disobedience much more notable. The author identifies Jonah with the eighth century prophet in Northern Israel (2 Kgs 14:23–25).

9. Hebrew uses the infinitive construct form of אמר with the preposition לְ to introduce direct speech (lit. "to say"; idiomatic usage); it is usually translated as "saying."

VERSE 2

Hebrew Text and Translation:

קוּם לֵךְ אֶל־נִינְוֵה הָעִיר הַגְּדוֹלָה וּקְרָא עָלֶיהָ
כִּי־עָלְתָה רָעָתָם לְפָנָי׃

"Arise, go to Nineveh, the great city, and proclaim against it, for their wickedness has come up before me."

Grammatical Analysis:

קוּם	Qal, imperative, second-person, masculine, singular (קוּם, to arise)
לֵךְ	Qal, imperative, second-person, masculine, singular (הָלַךְ, to go, walk)
אֶל	preposition, "to" or "towards"

Jonah Flees

נִינְוֵה	proper noun, "Nineveh"
הָעִיר	noun, feminine, singular, absolute (עִיר, city), with definite article
הַגְּדוֹלָה	adjective, feminine, singular, absolute (גָּדוֹל, great), with definite article
וּקְרָא	Qal, imperative, second-person, masculine, singular (קָרָא, to cry, call, proclaim, read), with conjunction
עָלֶיהָ	preposition, "against," with pronominal suffix (third-person, feminine, singular)
כִּי	conjunction, "because" or "that"
עָלְתָה	Qal, perfect, third-person, feminine, singular (עָלָה, to ascend, come up)
רָעָתָם	noun, feminine, singular, absolute (רָעָה, distress, calamity, evil), with pronominal suffix (third-person, masculine, plural)
לְפָנָי	regarded as a preposition (lit. "to my faces," from פָּנִים), with pronominal suffix (first-person, common, singular)

Exegetical Notes:

1. The word of the Lord to Jonah comprises a commission to go to Nineveh and cry out against the evil of the city. The three commands ("get up," "go," and "cry out") in quick succession underscore the urgency of the commission. The first two commands קוּם לֵךְ ("get up" and "go") were also given to Elijah when he was commissioned to go to Zarephath in the region of Sidon, to find refuge under the roof of a gentile woman (1 Kgs 17:9).

2. The expression הָעִיר הַגְּדוֹלָה is grammatically in apposition to "Nineveh" and highlights the importance of the city. The adjective גָּדוֹל may refer to the magnitude of the city or to its importance. According to the genealogical record in Gen

10, Nineveh was founded by Nimrod and is also there identified as "the great city" (Gen 10:8–12). Nineveh was one of the greatest cities in the ancient world. The archaeological site extends to 750 hectares.[5] The adjective "great" occurs fourteen times in the book of Jonah (1:2, 4, 10, 12, 16, 17; 3:2, 3, 5, 7; 4:1, 6, 11) and conveys to the reader that the book deals with weighty matters.

3. The third command קְרָא expresses the main task of Jonah's commission: he must get up and go to Nineveh to preach against the evil of the city. The verb occurs eight times in the book; it is used with different nuances but mainly relates to proclamation (Jonah 1:2, 6, 14; 2:2; 3:2, 4, 5, 8). The preposition עַל carries the hostile sense of "against."

4. It is interesting to note that the Septuagint changes the prepositional phrase "preach against it" to "preach in it" (καὶ κήρυξον ἐν αὐτῇ).

5. We may note here that the main task of a prophet was to proclaim (קְרָא) the word of the Lord. The word translated as "prophet" in our Bible simply means "spokesman" and does not necessarily relate to predictions of the future. Therefore, it is interesting to note that in Targum Jonathan, the Hebrew קְרָא (to proclaim) is rendered as אִתְנַבֵּי (to prophesy). The Jewish rabbis did not see a distinction between "to proclaim" and "to prophesy."[6]

---

5. Nineveh is located in upper Mesopotamia on the eastern bank of the Tigris River and is marked by the modern city of Mosul in Iraq. Two large tells, Tell Kuyunjiq and Tell Nabī Yūnus (the latter is named after the prophet Jonah), are the primary features of the site. Austen Henry Layard surveyed the site in 1847 and discovered the famous Royal Library of Ashurbanipal, which contained thousands of cuneiform clay tablets. The ancient site covers a large area of 750 hectares with a city wall of about twelve kilometers in circumference dating to 700 BC. It was destroyed in 612 BC by the Babylonians in accordance with the prophecy of Nahum. There is also an ancient shrine to commemorate the prophet Jonah at the site.

6. Targum Jonathan is an Aramaic translation of the Prophets in the Hebrew Bible.

Jonah Flees

6. The conjunction כִּי may either introduce a causal clause ("because") or an object clause that introduces indirect speech ("that").[7] It either provides the reason Jonah must preach against the city or gives the content of Jonah's message. We understand the conjunction as introducing a causal clause, since the clause is addressed to Jonah, intending to spur him on to action. Later in chapter 3 the content of Jonah's message is "Still forty days, and Nineveh will be overturned" (Jonah 3:4).

7. The last clause indicates the reason the Lord commissions Jonah to go to Nineveh: "Their evil has come up before me."[8] The third-person plural masculine suffix "their" indicates that the problem does not lie with the city as a social institution but with the wickedness of the people. According to Chisholm, "The antecedent of the plural suffix is implied, but not stated... the presence of the inhabitants is implied in the reference to the city."[9] The expression points toward the holiness of the Lord and emphasizes that the Lord holds people accountable for their actions. Yahweh is not just the God of Israel but also the judge of the entire world. About one hundred years later, the seventh century prophet Nahum provided a vivid description of Nineveh's wickedness (Nah 3:1–17).

8. The term רָעָה carries a range of nuances. It generally refers to something that is not good and may be translated as "bad" (2 Kgs 2:19), "calamity" (Esth 8:6; Isa 47:11; Ezek 7:5), "distress" or "affliction" (Ps 34:20; Prov 25:20), and "evil" or "wickedness" (Gen 50:20; 1 Sam 12:17; Jer 7:12). The context

---

7. Ferreira, *Old Testament Hebrew*, 20.

8. The Assyrians were notoriously cruel. Their cruel treatment of enemies is graphically displayed on the murals of the famous bronze Balawat gates, an Assyrian city around twenty-five kilometers southeast of Nineveh. Among other things the murals depict the horrific mutilation of captives by the Assyrians. These gates can be seen in the British Museum.

9. Chisholm, *Workbook for Intermediate Hebrew*, 26.

determines the precise meaning of a word. Here it refers to the evil behavior of the inhabitants of Nineveh.

VERSE 3

Hebrew Text and Translation:

וַיָּקָם יוֹנָה לִבְרֹחַ תַּרְשִׁישָׁה מִלִּפְנֵי יְהוָה וַיֵּרֶד יָפוֹ
וַיִּמְצָא אֳנִיָּה ׀ בָּאָה תַרְשִׁישׁ וַיִּתֵּן שְׂכָרָהּ
וַיֵּרֶד בָּהּ לָבוֹא עִמָּהֶם תַּרְשִׁישָׁה מִלִּפְנֵי יְהוָה׃

But Jonah rose to flee to Tarshish away from the presence of the LORD. So, he went down to Joppa, and after he found a ship which was about to go to Tarshish, he paid the fare (lit. its price), and then he went down into it to go with them to Tarshish away from the presence of the LORD.

Grammatical Analysis:

וַיָּקָם	Qal, imperfect *waw*-consecutive, 3rd person, masculine, singular (קוּם, to arise)
יוֹנָה	proper name, "Jonah" (alternative meaning, "dove")
לִבְרֹחַ	Qal, infinitive, construct (בָּרַח, to flee)
תַּרְשִׁישָׁה	proper noun, "Tarshish," with directional ה
מִלִּפְנֵי	preposition לִפְנֵי ("before"), with preposition מִן
יְהוָה	proper name, "Yahweh," or conventionally "the LORD"
וַיֵּרֶד	Qal, imperfect *waw*-consecutive, third-person, masculine, singular (יָרַד, to go down, to descend)
יָפוֹ	proper name, "Joppa"
וַיִּמְצָא	Qal, imperfect *waw*-consecutive, third-person, masculine, singular (מָצָא, to find)
אֳנִיָּה	noun, feminine, singular, absolute (אֳנִיָּה, ship)

Jonah Flees

בָּאָה	Qal, participle, active, feminine, singular (בּוֹא, to come, go)
תַרְשִׁישׁ	proper noun, "Tarshish"
וַיִּתֵּן	Qal, imperfect *waw*-consecutive, third-person, masculine, singular (נָתַן, to give)
שְׂכָרָהּ	noun, masculine, singular, construct (שָׂכָר, hire, wages, fare), with pronominal suffix (third-person, feminine, singular)
וַיֵּרֶד	Qal, imperfect *waw*-consecutive, third-person, masculine, singular (יָרַד, to go down, descend)
בָּהּ	preposition בְּ, with pronominal suffix (third-person, feminine, singular)
לָבוֹא	Qal, infinitive, construct (בּוֹא, to come, go), with preposition לְ
עִמָּהֶם	preposition עִם, with pronominal suffix (third-person, masculine, plural)
תַרְשִׁישָׁה	proper noun, "Tarshish," with directional ה
מִלִּפְנֵי	preposition לִפְנֵי ("before"), with preposition מִן
יְהוָה	proper name, "Yahweh," or conventionally "the LORD"

Exegetical Notes:

1. The response of Jonah takes the reader by surprise. Instead of obeying the command of the Lord, Jonah flees in the opposite direction. We may, therefore, translate the conjunction ו with the adversative "but" to bring out the contrast between the Lord's command and the prophet's action.

2. The infinitive construct לִבְרֹחַ (to flee) represents a purpose clause and expresses the reason for Jonah's getting up.

3. The prepositional phrase "away from the presence of the LORD" (מִלִּפְנֵי יְהוָה) is repeated twice to emphasize Jonah's intention.

The Book of Jonah

4. Note that the preposition מִן may indicate separation, meaning "away from."[10] It is important to observe that this expression often denotes geographical distance (cf. Gen 25:18; 27:30; 41:46), but it may also refer to spiritual separation or indicate a broken relationship (cf. Gen 3:8; 4:16; 36:6; Lev 22:3). While it may appear to the reader that Jonah is naïve and tries to outrun the Lord, we later learn from Jonah that his action was a demonstration of rebellion (cf. Jonah 4:2).

5. The *ethnak* (or *atnah*) accent under the proper name "LORD" indicates the major break in the verse (according to the Masoretic scribes) and so we place the full-stop after the proper noun.[11]

6. Also note the use of the verb יָרַד ("to go down"). Jonah resided in Gath Hepher[12] in Galilee which was located on a hill four hundred meters above sea level. One must go down from there to reach the seaport at Joppa.[13] The author is familiar with the topography of the land.

7. After finding a ship bound for Tarshish,[14] Jonah went down into it, and during the storm descended still deeper into the recesses of the ship (verse 5). The author uses the verb יָרַד ("to go down") not only to indicate physical descent but also to describe Jonah's spiritual condition (cf. Ps 22:29; 28:1; 30:3,

---

10. Ferreira, *Old Testament Hebrew*, 28.
11. Ferreira, *Old Testament Hebrew*, 12.
12. Jerome, who lived in Israel in the fourth century, mentioned that Gath Hepher was about three kilometers from Sepphoris on the road to Tiberius and that was "where Jonah's tomb can be seen." See Sheck, *Commentaries on the Twelve Prophets*, 245. Archaeological excavations have unearthed architectural remains from the time of Jonah.
13. Joppa was one of the major ports of ancient Israel. Recent excavations have revealed Egyptian fortifications from the Late Bronze Age (1500–1200 BC).
14. Several locations for Tarshish have been suggested over the years. See Day, *From Creation to Babel*, 54–165. Most likely, the Tarshish in the book of Jonah refers to a place in southern Spain, which was the farthermost western frontier of the known world at the time. Precious metals, like silver and gold, and exotic animals were imported from there to the Middle East.

Jonah Flees

9; 55:15; 88:4; 107:26; 115:17; 143:7). Fleeing from the presence of the Lord only increases gloom and despair.

8. Note the directive הָ, "towards Tarshish." According to Snaith, "'To Tarshish' stands for 'to the farthest west', i.e., to the ends of the earth."[15] Jonah did not only ignore the Lord's command but rebelled against it by travelling in the opposite direction. The comment in the NET Bible is perceptive: "On one level, Jonah was attempting to avoid a disagreeable task, but the narrator's description personalizes Jonah's rejection of the task. Jonah's issue is with the Lord Himself, not just his commission."[16]

9. We may also translate the subsequent two clauses as "so he went down to Joppa and found a ship."

10. Note the use of the participle בָּאָה. The Hebrew participle may express an action that is about to take place.[17] Hence, we may translate the expression as "he ... found a ship about to go to Tarshish ..." It is important to note the placement of the accent on the last syllable of the verb. The Masoretic scribes placed the accent on the last syllable to distinguish the form of the participle from the perfect tense which takes the accent on the first syllable.

11. We may translate the last two clauses as "after he bought a ticket (lit. after he gave its price),[18] he went down into it ..."

12. Note the preposition with the pronominal suffix עִמָּהֶם, "with them." Later we will learn that the sailors of the ship were gentile polytheists.

---

15. Snaith, *Notes on the Hebrew Text of Jonah*, 9.
16. *NET Bible*, 1712.
17. Ferreira, *Old Testament Hebrew*, 40.
18. On the use of the verb "to give" (נָתַן), Chisholm makes the following comment, "It occasionally refers to placing a purchase price or wage into another's hand and can be translated 'pay.'" See Chisholm, *Workbook for Intermediate Hebrew*, 29.

The Book of Jonah

VERSE 4

Hebrew Text and Translation:

וַיהוָ֗ה הֵטִ֤יל רֽוּחַ־גְּדוֹלָה֙ אֶל־הַיָּ֔ם וַיְהִ֥י סַֽעַר־גָּד֖וֹל בַּיָּ֑ם וְהָ֣אֳנִיָּ֔ה חִשְּׁבָ֖ה לְהִשָּׁבֵֽר׃

But the LORD hurled a great wind on the sea so that there was a great storm on the sea, and consequently, the ship was about to break up (lit. the ship was thinking about disintegrating or being smashed into pieces).

Grammatical Analysis:

וַיהוָה	proper name, "Yahweh," or conventionally "the LORD," with the conjunction
הֵטִיל	Hifil, imperfect, third-person, masculine, singular (טוּל, to hurl, cast)
רוּחַ	noun, masculine, singular, absolute (רוּחַ, wind, spirit, breath)
גְּדוֹלָה	adjective, feminine, singular, absolute (גָּדוֹל, great)
אֶל	preposition
הַיָּם	noun, masculine, singular, absolute (יָם, sea), with the definite article
וַיְהִי	Qal, imperfect *waw*-consecutive, third-person, masculine, singular (הָיָה, to be, become, is)
סַעַר	noun, masculine, singular, absolute (סַעַר, storm)
גָּדוֹל	adjective, masculine, singular, absolute (גָּדוֹל, great)
בַּיָּם	noun, masculine, singular, absolute (יָם, sea), with the definite article, and preposition בְּ
וְהָאֳנִיָּה	noun, feminine, singular, absolute (אֳנִיָּה, ship), with the definite article, and with the conjunction

Jonah Flees

חִשְּׁבָה   Piel, perfect, third-person, feminine, singular (חָשַׁב, to think)

לְהִשָּׁבֵר   Nifal, infinitive, construct (שָׁבַר, to break in pieces), with preposition לְ

Exegetical Notes:

1. In verse 4, the subject is placed before the verb and the tense reverts to the perfect, breaking the line of narration with the *waw*-imperfect consecutive. The change in the syntactical pattern signals a major theological point of the author. The line of narration is broken because the Lord has broken onto the scene. The subject is placed before the verb to highlight that God can and does break into history to compel natural phenomena to accomplish his salvific purposes. The imperfect changes to a perfect to indicate that while Jonah was travelling to Joppa and preparing for his voyage to escape his commission, God was already preparing the storm to curtail Jonah's flight to Tarshish. God is always one step ahead of human schemes, knowing the end from the beginning.

2. The Hifil הֵטִיל (to hurl or to cast), which ordinarily expresses causative action, underscores that God caused the storm on the sea through a great wind. God uses means to control the forces of nature, but the means themselves are directly governed by God. The verb הֵטִיל occurs four times in the chapter (Jonah 1:4, 5, 12, 15).

3. It is interesting to note that instead of the LORD "hurling" a wind upon the sea, the Septuagint has the LORD "raising up" a wind upon the sea (καὶ κύριος ἐξήγειρεν πνεῦμα εἰς τὴν θάλασσαν).

4. Note that the direct object of the verb (רוּחַ־גְּדוֹלָה) is anarthrous (it does not have an article and therefore is indefinite). The LORD hurled "a great wind" on the sea, i.e., it was not a regular wind—a seasonal or expected wind—rather, it was an abnormal or unexpected wind.

The Book of Jonah

5. "Sea" (יָם) is also an important word in the chapter, occurring eleven times (Jonah 1:4, 5, 9, 11, 12, 13, 15). In Scripture, the seas may function as a symbol of punishment and judgment (cf. Exod 10:19; 14:16, 26; 15:1). Those opposing the will of the Lord will soon find themselves in very unstable and precarious situations.

6. Also observe that in the final clause of the sentence the subject ("ship") is placed before the verb, which serves to highlight the effect of the storm upon the ship. The personification "the ship thought to be broken" draws the reader into the predicament of the ship. Most translations do not reflect the personification here, which ". . . fails to capture the literary dimension of the story or the dramatic effect the narrator intended."[19] The term שָׁבֵר is commonly used for a shipwreck in the Hebrew Bible (1 Kgs 22:48; 2 Chr 20:37; Ezek 27:34; Ps 48:7).

VERSE 5

Hebrew Text and Translation:

וַיִּירְאוּ הַמַּלָּחִים וַיִּזְעֲקוּ אִישׁ אֶל־אֱלֹהָיו וַיָּטִלוּ אֶת־הַכֵּלִים
אֲשֶׁר בָּאֳנִיָּה אֶל־הַיָּם לְהָקֵל מֵעֲלֵיהֶם
וְיוֹנָה יָרַד אֶל־יַרְכְּתֵי הַסְּפִינָה וַיִּשְׁכַּב וַיֵּרָדַם׃

Then the sailors became afraid, and every man cried to his gods, and they threw the cargo which was in the ship into the sea to lighten it for them (lit. from around them). In the meantime, Jonah had gone below into the hold of the ship and laid down and fallen into a deep sleep.

---

19. Chisholm, *Workbook for Intermediate Hebrew*, 33.

Jonah Flees

Grammatical Analysis:

וַיִּֽירְאוּ	Qal, imperfect *waw*-consecutive, third-person, masculine, plural (יָרֵא, to fear)
הַמַּלָּחִים	noun, masculine, plural, absolute (מַלָּח, mariner, sailor), with the definite article
וַֽיִּזְעֲקוּ	Qal, imperfect *waw*-consecutive, third-person, masculine, plural (זָעַק, to cry out)
אִישׁ	noun, masculine, singular, absolute (אִישׁ, man, each)
אֶל	preposition
אֱלֹהָיו	noun, masculine, plural, construct (אֱלֹהִים, God, gods), with pronominal suffix (third-person, masculine, singular)
וַיָּטִלוּ	Hifil, imperfect *waw*-consecutive, third-person, masculine, plural (טוּל, to hurl, cast)
אֶת	direct object marker
הַכֵּלִים	noun, masculine, plural, absolute (כְּלִי, article, utensil, vessel), with the definite article
אֲשֶׁר	relative pronoun
בָּאֳנִיָּה	noun, feminine, singular, absolute (אֳנִיָּה, ship), with the preposition בְּ, and with the definite article
אֶל	preposition
הַיָּם	noun, masculine, singular, absolute (יָם, sea), with the definite article
לְהָקֵל	Hifil, infinitive, construct (קָלַל, to make light, lighten), with the preposition לְ
מֵעֲלֵיהֶם	preposition עַל, with the preposition מִן, and with the pronominal suffix (third-person, masculine, plural)
וְיוֹנָה	proper name, "Jonah" (alternative meaning, "dove"), with the conjunction וְ

יָרַד	Qal, perfect, third-person, masculine, singular (יָרַד, to go down, descend)
אֶל	preposition
יַרְכְּתֵי	noun, feminine, dual, construct (יַרְכָה, side, recess, innermost part)
הַסְּפִינָה	noun, feminine, singular, absolute (סְפִינָה, vessel, ship), with the definite article
וַיִּשְׁכַּב	Qal, imperfect *waw*-consecutive, third-person, masculine, singular (שָׁכַב, to lie down)
וַיֵּרָדַם	Nifal, imperfect *waw*-consecutive, third-person, masculine, singular (רָדַם, to fall into a deep sleep)

Exegetical Notes:

1. The depiction of the sailors' reaction to the storm is realistic and full of sympathy. Their fear is a normal reaction to the imminent threat and communicates to the reader that they faced an extraordinary storm. This terrifying danger compelled them to pray to their gods. Although they were common sailors, they believed in the gods and knew how to pray. The text also reveals here that the sailors were gentiles since the Israelites worshiped the LORD. These gentile sailors not only prayed, but they also proceeded to lighten the ship by throwing its cargo into the sea. They did everything according to their knowledge and ability to save the lives of those on the ship. They instinctively recognized that human life was much more valuable than the mercantile intentions of their voyage.

2. The noun אִישׁ is here used in a distributive sense (i.e., the term refers to individual members of the group, "everyone" or "each one").

3. It is unlikely that the plural of the term אֱלֹהִים is a "plural of majesty" and that it implies "god" in the singular; it rather

reflects the polytheism of the sailors.[20] However, the Septuagint translates the Hebrew אֱלֹהִים with the singular τὸν θεὸν.

4. The word cargo (כֵּלִים) in the plural refers to the different items that the ship was transporting.[21]

5. However, in the meantime, Jonah had gone down into the ship and was fast asleep. The line of narration consisting of *waw*-imperfect consecutives is again broken, and the subject is placed before the verb (יָרַד). The perfect (יָרַד) introduces a circumstantial clause (i.e., "meanwhile..."), indicating a literary flashback.[22] While the sailors did their best to save the ship and human life, Jonah withdrew himself from the situation. Although Jonah was the cause of their predicament, he stayed completely passive. The subject of the sentence, Jonah, is placed before the verb to highlight the contrast between the sailors' behavior and that of Jonah. While everyone was busy, the prophet Jonah went into the inner recess of the ship to lie down and sleep.

6. The term for ship here, סְפִינָה, is a *hapax legomena* (i.e., the word occurs only once in the Hebrew Bible). The root ספף refers to a cover of some kind, and so the term סְפִינָה was used to refer to a ship with a deck (a covered hold). The term is probably used here instead of the more common אֳנִיָּה to highlight the different decks of the ship.[23]

7. In the lower deck of the ship Jonah laid down and then fell into a deep sleep. The two imperfect *waw*-consecutive verbs

---

20. Echols, *Reading Jonah*, 9–10.
21. Chisholm, *Workbook for Intermediate Hebrew*, 35.
22. Ferreira, *Old Testament Hebrew*, 50–51.
23. The discovery of the 2,400-year-old Ma'agan Michael Ship off the coast of Israel in 1985 provides a vivid example of the kind of ship that Jonah might have used to flee his commission. The reconstructed ship is 16.6 meters long and 4.3 meters wide, with a displacement of about twenty-three tons. A cargo of thirteen tons of stone building material and seventy ceramic pots were found around the wreck. The ship would have had a crew of around ten to fifteen sailors. The wreck is displayed in the Hecht Museum at the University of Haifa.

instead of a simple infinitive to express purpose portrays Jonah as being dazed (stupefied) by the situation. The Nifal וַיֵּרָדַם indicates that sleep overcame him. The prophet's response is not natural; it appears he was out of touch with his surroundings due to the gravity of the situation and he entered into a state of depression.

VERSE 6

Hebrew Text and Translation:

וַיִּקְרַב אֵלָיו רַב הַחֹבֵל וַיֹּאמֶר לוֹ מַה־לְּךָ נִרְדָּם
קוּם קְרָא אֶל־אֱלֹהֶיךָ אוּלַי יִתְעַשֵּׁת הָאֱלֹהִים לָנוּ וְלֹא נֹאבֵד׃

So, the captain approached him and said to him, "What are you doing, sleeping? Arise, call on your god. Perhaps this God may show Himself mindful of us, so that we may not perish."

Grammatical Analysis:

וַיִּקְרַב	Qal, imperfect *waw*-consecutive, third-person, masculine, plural (קָרַב, to approach, come near)
אֵלָיו	preposition אֶל, with pronominal suffix (third-person, common, singular)
רַב	noun, masculine, singular, construct (רַב, chief)
הַחֹבֵל	noun, masculine, plural, absolute (חֹבֵל, sailor), with the definite article
וַיֹּאמֶר	Qal, imperfect *waw*-consecutive, third-person, masculine, plural (אָמַר, to say)
לוֹ	preposition לְ, with pronominal suffix (third-person, masculine, singular)
מַה	adverb, "what?"

Jonah Flees

לְךָ	preposition לְ, with pronominal suffix (second-person, masculine, singular)
נִרְדָּם	Nifal, participle, active, masculine, singular, absolute (רָדַם, to fall into a deep sleep)
קוּם	Qal, imperative, second-person, masculine, singular (קוּם to arise)
קְרָא	Qal, imperative, second-person, masculine, singular (קָרָא, to cry, call, proclaim, read)
אֶל	preposition
אֱלֹהֶיךָ	noun, masculine, plural, absolute (אֵל, God), with pronominal suffix (second-person, masculine, singular)
אוּלַי	adverb, "perhaps"
יִתְעַשֵּׁת	Hithpael, imperfect, third-person, masculine, singular (עָשַׁת, to think, consider)
הָאֱלֹהִים	noun, masculine, plural, absolute (אֵל, God), with the definite article
לָנוּ	preposition לְ, with pronominal suffix (first-person, common, plural)
וְלֹא	adverb "not," with the conjunction
נֹאבֵד	Qal, imperfect, first-person, common, plural (אָבַד, to perish)

Exegetical Notes:

1. The captain of the ship (the chief of the sailors) finds Jonah and rebukes him for sleeping.[24] The first of the two nouns in construct relationship, רַב, expresses the principal idea. Jonah is urged to pray to his god. There is nothing more that could be done to secure the safety of the ship except to pray for

---

[24]. This rebuke to stir Jonah up to action is in fact an act of grace. One of the best remedies for depression is activity.

divine assistance. The participle (נִרְדָּם) may indicate continuous action.[25]

2. The adverb אוּלַי ("perhaps") indicates that the captain is not certain that Jonah's god would save them but is hopeful that Jonah's god is the God (הָאֱלֹהִים) that will pity them. The article with God is best understood as a demonstrative "this." We may conjecture that the captain, who probably spoke Aramaic or Phoenician, had a less-than-perfect command of Hebrew.

3. Note the interesting use of the Hithpael, יִתְעַשֵּׁת, "perhaps this God may show Himself mindful of us." According to Snaith, "The force of the Hithpael can be retained with 'perhaps God will bethink Himself for our benefit.'"[26] The verb עָשַׁת is a *hapax legomena*. Some scholars have conjectured that the use of this verb is an Aramaism and that it shows that the book is late. However, since our knowledge of ancient Hebrew is limited and the "Aramaism" is on the tongue of these gentile sailors, we cannot infer anything specific about the dating of the book of Jonah based on this observation. It is also interesting to note that the Septuagint and the Peshitta translated the term as "save."[27]

4. וְלֹא נֹאבֵד is a key expression in the book of Jonah which is used to highlight one of the important themes of the book (Jonah 1:6, 14; 3:9). According to Limburg, "The Jonah story deals with matters of life and death. Three times that concern is expressed . . ."[28]

---

25. Ferreira, *Old Testament Hebrew*, 40.
26. Snaith, *Notes on the Hebrew Text of Jonah*, 15.
27. Snaith, *Notes on the Hebrew Text of Jonah*, 15.
28. Limburg, *Jonah*, 51.

Jonah Flees

VERSE 7

Hebrew Text and Translation:

וַיֹּאמְרוּ אִישׁ אֶל־רֵעֵהוּ לְכוּ וְנַפִּילָה גוֹרָלוֹת
וְנֵדְעָה בְּשֶׁלְּמִי הָרָעָה הַזֹּאת לָנוּ וַיַּפִּלוּ גּוֹרָלוֹת
וַיִּפֹּל הַגּוֹרָל עַל־יוֹנָה׃

Then each man said to his friend, "Come, let us cast lots so we may know on whose account (because of whom) this calamity has come upon us." So, they cast lots and the lot fell on Jonah.

Grammatical Analysis:

וַיֹּאמְרוּ	Qal, imperfect *waw*-consecutive, third-person, masculine, plural (אָמַר, to say)
אִישׁ	noun, masculine, singular, absolute (אִישׁ, man, each)
אֶל	preposition
רֵעֵהוּ	noun, masculine, singular, construct (רֵעַ, friend, companion), with pronominal suffix (third-person, masculine, singular)
לְכוּ	Qal, imperative, second-person, masculine, singular (הָלַךְ, to go, walk)
וְנַפִּילָה	Hifil, imperfect (cohortative), first-person, common, plural (נָפַל, to fall), with conjunction
גוֹרָלוֹת	noun, feminine, plural, absolute (גּוֹרָל, lot)
וְנֵדְעָה	Qal, imperfect (cohortative), first-person, common, plural (יָדַע, to know), with conjunction וְ
בְּשֶׁלְּמִי	shorter form of the relative pronoun שֶׁ (אֲשֶׁר), with preposition בְּ, with preposition לְ, with adverb מִי
הָרָעָה	noun, feminine, singular, absolute (רָעָה, bad, evil), with the definite article

הַזֹּאת	demonstrative pronoun זֹאת (feminine, singular), with the article
לָנוּ	preposition לְ, with pronominal suffix (first-person, common, plural)
וַיַּפִּלוּ	Hifil, imperfect *waw*-consecutive, first-person, common, plural (נָפַל, to fall)
גּוֹרָלוֹת	noun, feminine, plural, absolute (גּוֹרָל, lot)
וַיִּפֹּל	Qal, imperfect *waw*-consecutive, third-person, masculine, singular (נָפַל, to fall)
הַגּוֹרָל	noun, feminine, singular, absolute (גּוֹרָל, lot), with the definite article
עַל	preposition
יוֹנָה	proper name, "Jonah" (alternative meaning, "dove")

Exegetical Notes:

1. The narrator leaves Jonah and returns to the sailors. The sailors perceive that the storm is extraordinary and that there may be a divine intention behind it.

2. Again, the noun אִישׁ is used in a distributive sense (i.e., the term refers to individual members of the group, "everyone" or "each one").

3. The expression אִישׁ אֶל־רֵעֵהוּ ("each man to his friend") is redundant in the Hebrew line of narration, but the author adds it to depict the humanity and camaraderie that exist among the sailors—they are friends and discuss the crisis with one another.

4. The three imperatives (in Hebrew the imperative is followed by two cohortatives) show the decisiveness of the sailors; they are men of action and practicality. We may translate the conjunction before the final cohortative as introducing a purpose

clause, "in order that."²⁹ The sailors try to ascertain the reason for their predicament by casting lots, which was a form of divination in the ancient world. However, from Proverbs we know that the apparent chance outcome of the lot is also under divine control (Prov 16:33).

5. Note that the term בְּשֶׁלְמִי is a compound word comprising of four elements. The consonant בּ represents the preposition בְּ, the syllable שֶׁ is an abbreviation for the relative pronoun אֲשֶׁר, the consonant ל is the inseparable preposition לְ, and מִי is the interrogative pronoun "who."³⁰ In other words, combining all the elements together, we get "because of whom" (lit. because of whom to whom).

6. According to Snaith, "The שׁ is N. Israelite for אֲשֶׁר; it appears in Rabbinic Hebrew, and in the *daleth* of Syriac and Aramaic."³¹ The use of the particle שׁ supports the northern provenance of the book of Jonah.

VERSE 8

Hebrew Text and Translation:

וַיֹּאמְרוּ אֵלָיו הַגִּידָה־נָּא לָנוּ בַּאֲשֶׁר לְמִי־הָרָעָה הַזֹּאת לָנוּ מַה־מְּלַאכְתְּךָ וּמֵאַיִן תָּבוֹא מָה אַרְצֶךָ וְאֵי־מִזֶּה עַם אָתָּה׃

Then they said to him, "Tell us, now! On whose account *has* this calamity *come upon* us? What is your occupation? And where do you come from? What is your country? And of what people are you?"

---

29. Ferreira, *Old Testament Hebrew*, 36.

30. The particle שׁ is mostly seen in the language of Northern Israel for אֲשֶׁר (e.g., Judg 5:7; 6:17; 7:12; 8:26; 2 Kgs 6:11). It was probably adopted by Hebrew speakers in the north through the influence of Aramaic.

31. Snaith, *Notes on the Hebrew Text of Jonah*, 17.

The Book of Jonah

Grammatical Analysis:

וַיֹּאמְרוּ	Qal, imperfect *waw*-consecutive, third-person, masculine, plural (אָמַר, to say)
אֵלָיו	preposition, with pronominal suffix (third-person, masculine, singular)
הַגִּידָה	Hifil, imperative, second-person, masculine, singular (נָגַד, to tell, declare)
נָא	particle of entreaty
לָנוּ	preposition לְ, with pronominal suffix (first-person, common, plural)
בַּאֲשֶׁר	relative pronoun אֲשֶׁר, with preposition בְּ
לְמִי	preposition לְ, with adverb מִי
הָרָעָה	noun, feminine, singular, absolute (רָעָה, bad, evil), with the definite article
הַזֹּאת	demonstrative pronoun זֹאת (feminine, singular), with the article
לָנוּ	preposition לְ, with pronominal suffix (first-person, common, plural)
מַה	adverb, "what?"
מְלַאכְתְּךָ	noun, feminine, singular, construct (מְלָאכָה, work, occupation), with pronominal suffix (second-person, masculine, singular)
וּמֵאַיִן	interrogative אַיִן, "where," with preposition מִן, and with conjunction וְ
תָּבוֹא	Qal, imperfect, second-person, masculine, singular (בּוֹא, to come, go)
מָה	adverb, "what?"
אַרְצֶךָ	noun, feminine, singular, construct (אֶרֶץ, land, earth, country), with pronominal suffix (second-person, masculine, singular)

Jonah Flees

וְאֵי	interrogative אַי ("where"), with conjunction וְ
מִזֶּה	demonstrative pronoun זֶה (masculine, singular), with preposition מִן
עַם	noun, masculine, singular, absolute (עַם, people, tribe)
אָתָּה	second personal pronoun, masculine, singular

Exegetical Notes:

1. It is important to observe the response of the sailors after the lot fell upon Jonah. They did not immediately conclude that the fault lay with Jonah but proceeded to inquire further. They did not put total trust in the outcome of the lot (divination) but took the outcome as a cue for further investigation. Instead of accusing Jonah, they inquired further. The portrayal of the sailors is consistently positive.

2. The Hebrew particle נָא ("now" or "please") conveys a sense of both urgency and politeness.

3. The sailors have five questions for Jonah: 1) On whose account has this calamity come upon us? 2) What is your occupation? 3) Where do you come from? 4) What is your country? 5) And of what people are you?

4. The term מְלָאכָה may either refer to Jonah's regular occupation or to the reason for this voyage.

5. Note that the pronoun אָתָּה ("you") is placed in an empathic position right at the end of the series of questions. The questions lead up to the final אָתָּה, placing the focus on Jonah and pressuring him to give an account of himself. Those who have done wrong are often questioned in the biblical text to lead them to acknowledgment of wrongdoing and repentance (e.g., Gen 3:9–11; 4:9–10; 26:10; 29:25; Judg 2:2; 1 Sam 13:11).

6. The verb בּוֹא occurs five times in Jonah (1:3, 8; 2:7; 3:4); it usually means "to come" or "to come in" from the reference

of the speaker but it may also mean "to go" or "to go in." Since it is preceded here by the adverb מֵאַיִן, it means "to come."

7. The word בְּשֶׁלְמִי is here separated into two parts: בַּאֲשֶׁר לְמִי (lit. "by whom" and "for whom").

VERSE 9

Hebrew Text and Translation:

וַיֹּאמֶר אֲלֵיהֶם עִבְרִי אָנֹכִי וְאֶת־יְהוָה אֱלֹהֵי הַשָּׁמַיִם אֲנִי יָרֵא אֲשֶׁר־עָשָׂה אֶת־הַיָּם וְאֶת־הַיַּבָּשָׁה׃

Then he said to them, "I am a Hebrew, and the LORD, the God of the heavens I am fearing, the one who made the sea and the dry land."

Grammatical Analysis:

וַיֹּאמֶר	Qal, imperfect *waw*-consecutive, third-person, masculine, singular (אָמַר, to say)
אֲלֵיהֶם	preposition, with pronominal suffix (third-person, masculine, plural)
עִבְרִי	noun, singular, absolute (עִבְרִי, Hebrew)
אָנֹכִי	first personal pronoun, common, singular
וְאֶת	direct object marker, with conjunction וְ
יְהוָה	proper name, "Yahweh," or conventionally "the LORD"
אֱלֹהֵי	noun, masculine, plural, construct (אֵל, God)
הַשָּׁמַיִם	noun, masculine, dual, absolute (שָׁמַיִם, heavens), with the definite article
אֲנִי	first personal pronoun, common, singular
יָרֵא	Qal, participle, active, masculine, singular (יָרֵא, to fear)[32]

32. The analysis of this word differs among scholars. Some regard it as a

Jonah Flees

אֲשֶׁר	relative pronoun
עָשָׂה	Qal, perfect, third-person, masculine, singular (עָשָׂה, to do, make)
אֶת	direct object marker
הַיָּם	noun, masculine, singular, absolute (יָם, sea), with the definite article
וְאֶת	direct object marker, with conjunction וְ
הַיַּבָּשָׁה	noun, feminine, singular, absolute (יַבָּשָׁה, dry land), with the definite article

Exegetical Notes:

1. In this verse we have Jonah's confession of faith.

2. Jonah answers only the last question directly, "Of what people are you?," which is perhaps the most important one. He says, "I am a Hebrew." In the Hebrew text, עִבְרִי אָנֹכִי is a noun sentence, with the predicate placed before the subject, thereby emphasising the predicate.[33] We note that the personal pronoun is the longer form אָנֹכִי, which also often carries more emphasis than the shorter form אֲנִי. Jonah is proud to be a Hebrew and is quite forthright with his public testimony.[34]

---

verbal adjective (See Davidson, *Analytical Hebrew and Chaldee Lexicon*, 344), whereas others regard it as the perfect tense of the verb "to fear" (See *The Blue Letter Bible* and Brown and Smith, *Reader's Hebrew Bible*, 1040). The term is not a verbal adjective here since it does not describe a noun in its context. The perfect tense, which usually indicates past action in narrative, also does not fit the context well (in addition, note that the grammatical person of the verb which would be third person does not agree with the subject which is first person). Regarding the term as a participle fits the context best; Jonah naturally identifies his faith with the words "I am fearing the LORD." Also, see Snaith, *Notes on the Hebrew Text of Jonah*, 18; and Chisholm, *Workbook for Intermediate Hebrew*, 44.

33. Ferreira, *Old Testament Hebrew*, 16.

34. Israel or the land of Canaan is also identified in Gen 40:15 as "the land of the Hebrews." Paul uses a similar expression in Phil 3:5, "*I am* a Hebrew born of Hebrews." In both of these instances, as in Jonah 1:9, the Hebrew

3. Interestingly, instead of "I am a Hebrew," the Septuagint has "I am the servant of the Lord" (Δοῦλος κυρίου ἐγώ). Most probably the translator of the Hebrew text confused the *resh* for a *daleth* in the Hebrew text and so translated "Hebrew" (עברי) as "servant" (עבדי). The *yodh* may have suggested the divine name to the translator. In other words, it is possible that the variant reading in the Septuagint may not represent a variant in the *Vorlage* but simply a misunderstanding of the text.[35] Or another possibility is that the translator is interpreting "Hebrew" as meaning a "servant of the LORD."

4. The description of Jonah as a "Hebrew" rather than as a "prophet" may reflect the intention of the author to portray Jonah as a representative of the Israelites in general.

5. After answering the last question, Jonah offers further information about his faith. The word order of the Hebrew sentence is again significant. The predicate "Yahweh, the God of the heavens" is placed before the verb for emphasis (the phrase אֱלֹהֵי הַשָּׁמַיִם is in apposition to Yahweh). It is noteworthy that the shorter form of the personal pronoun אֲנִי is now used instead of the longer form, the purpose being to place the emphasis on the God Jonah fears and not on Jonah himself.

6. We take יָרֵא to be a participle (Qal, masculine, singular), indicating continuous action (see footnote in the Grammatical Analysis).

7. Another description of the LORD is supplied by the relative clause, "who made the sea and the dry land." Tellingly, the term יַבָּשָׁה ("dry land") is used instead of אֶרֶץ ("earth") because the concern of the sailors at the moment is to get to the safety of dry land. The one that controls the world and provides the safety of the dry land is the same God Jonah worships. According to Limburg, "Whatever Jonah's problems may be, knowledge about the faith is not one of them! He can recite orthodox confessions and he knows how to

---

speaker is giving his testimony before gentiles in a polemical context.

35. See Snaith, *Notes on the Hebrew Text of Jonah*, 18.

Jonah Flees

pray."[36] Jonah's profession of God in universalistic terms fits well with the gentile context. The expression "God of heaven" was typical of the Persian period and occurs twenty times in the Old Testament (Gen 24:3, 7; 2 Chr 36:23; Neh 1:5; 2:4, 20; Ps 136:26; Jonah 1:9); twelve of them are in the Aramaic sections of Daniel and Ezra (Ezra 1:2; 5:11, 12; 6:9, 10; 7:12, 21, 23; Dan 2:18, 19, 28, 37, 44; and "the Lord of heaven" in Dan 5:23).

8. The term יַבָּשָׁה is also prominent in the creation narrative where God brings order out of chaos by limiting the distribution of the waters (Gen 1:9–10).

VERSE 10

Hebrew Text and Translation:

וַיִּירְא֤וּ הָאֲנָשִׁים֙ יִרְאָ֣ה גְדוֹלָ֔ה וַיֹּאמְר֥וּ אֵלָ֖יו מַה־זֹּ֣את עָשִׂ֑יתָ כִּֽי־יָדְע֣וּ הָאֲנָשִׁ֗ים כִּֽי־מִלִּפְנֵ֤י יְהוָה֙ ה֣וּא בֹרֵ֔חַ כִּ֥י הִגִּ֖יד לָהֶֽם׃

And so, the men feared greatly, and they said to him, "What is this that you have done?" For the men knew that from the presence of the LORD he was fleeing, because he had told them.

Grammatical Analysis:

וַיִּירְאוּ	Qal, imperfect *waw*-consecutive, third-person, masculine, plural (יָרֵא, to fear)
הָאֲנָשִׁים	noun, masculine, plural, absolute (אִישׁ, man), with the definite article
יִרְאָה	noun, feminine, singular, absolute (יִרְאָה, fear)
גְדוֹלָה	adjective, feminine, singular, absolute (גָּדוֹל, great)

---

36. Limburg, *Jonah*, 54.

The Book of Jonah

וַיֹּאמְרוּ	Qal, imperfect *waw*-consecutive, third-person, masculine, plural (אָמַר, to say)
אֵלָיו	preposition אֶל, with pronominal suffix (third-person, masculine, singular)
מַה	adverb, "what?"
זֹאת	demonstrative pronoun זֹאת (feminine, singular)
עָשִׂיתָ	Qal, perfect, second-person, masculine, singular (עָשָׂה, to do, make)
כִּי	conjunction, "because"
יָדְעוּ	Qal, perfect, third-person, common, plural (יָדַע, to know)
הָאֲנָשִׁים	noun, masculine, plural, absolute (אִישׁ, man), with the definite article
כִּי	conjunction, "because" or "that"
מִלִּפְנֵי	preposition לִפְנֵי ("before"), with preposition מִן
יְהוָה	proper name, "Yahweh," or conventionally "the LORD"
הוּא	third personal pronoun, masculine, singular
בֹּרֵחַ	Qal, participle, active, masculine, singular (בָּרַח, to flee)
כִּי	conjunction, "because"
הִגִּיד	Hifil, perfect, third-person, masculine, singular (נָגַד, to tell, declare)
לָהֶם	preposition לְ, with pronominal suffix (third-person, masculine, plural)

Exegetical Notes:

1. In this verse we note that Jonah had also made a confession of sin, albeit not to God but to the sailors. He acknowledged that he was disobeying the commission of the Lord by going to Tarshish.

Jonah Flees

2. Note that the sailors are now described as "the men" (הָאֲנָשִׁים). The term occurs five times in Jonah (1:10, 13, 16; 3:5). For the author, the sailors' actions and attitudes show that they are more than just unrefined labourers but are men that reflect the image of God.

3. We may translate the imperfect *waw*-consecutive as "Then the men feared..." In verse 5, the sailors only "feared," now they "feared greatly." Their fear for God is evidently greater than their fear of natural calamities. With the introduction of this spiritual element, they become more than simply sailors.

4. The response of the sailors or "the men" reveals a greater fear of God than that of the prophet Jonah who had just made a profession of God. The Hebrew text deepens their sense of fear by using the verb יָרֵא ("to fear") with its corresponding cognate accusative יִרְאָה ("fear") as well as the attributive adjective "great" (גְדוֹלָה).[37]

5. According to the NET Bible, "The verb יָרֵא (yare') has a broad range of meanings, including 'to fear, to worship, to revere, to respect'. When God is the object, it normally means 'to fear' or 'to worship.'"[38]

6. The men's question, "What is this that you have done?" derives from Jonah's admission that he was fleeing from the presence of the LORD. Note the two causal clauses introduced by the conjunction כִּי. The two verbs in the two causal clauses are both in the perfect tense since they describe actions prior to the main verbs in the line of narration, "they feared (וַיִּירְאוּ)... and they said (וַיֹּאמְרוּ)..." In English we often use the pluperfect to translate such circumstantial clauses, e.g., "because he had told them."

---

37. A cognate accusative in Hebrew refers to the situation where the object (which is presented in the accusative case) of the verb comes from the same verbal root (e.g., "He dreamed a dream."). A cognate accusative may sometimes be regarded or translated as an adverb in English (see Echols, *Reading Jonah*, 20).

38. *NET Bible*, 1714.

7. The important verb יָדַע implies that the men gained spiritual insight into God's will, albeit through the Israelite prophet Jonah.

8. The question "What is this that you have done?" also occurs in Gen 3:13, where God questions the woman after she ate the forbidden fruit. The question is used in the context of deception when the affronted party is not pleased with the offender (also cf. Gen 12:18; 26:10; 29:25; Exod 14:11; Judg 15:11). Here the question is perhaps more an exclamation of surprise at Jonah's disobedience rather than a real question.

9. According to Echols, "There may be paronomasia (word play) with the previous verse, since this verb rather than ברא ("to create") appears there as well: YHWH 'עשׂה' the sea and the dry land, but Jonah 'עשׂה' rebellion."[39]

10. The participle בֹרֵחַ indicates continuing action. Jonah was still in the process of fleeing from God. The pronoun הוּא ("he") is pleonastic for emphasis.[40]

VERSE 11

Hebrew Text and Translation:

וַיֹּאמְרוּ אֵלָיו מַה־נַּעֲשֶׂה לָּךְ וְיִשְׁתֹּק הַיָּם מֵעָלֵינוּ
כִּי הַיָּם הוֹלֵךְ וְסֹעֵר׃

So, they said to him, "What should we do with you in order that the sea may become calm from upon us?"—for the sea was becoming increasingly stormy (lit. the sea was continuously rushing and raging).

---

39. Echols, *Reading Jonah*, 20.

40. Pleonasm is a literary device that describes the use of more words than are required to express a meaning. The extra word or words are not necessarily superfluous but are added for emphasis (e.g., "I heard it with my own ears").

Jonah Flees

Grammatical Analysis:

וַיֹּאמְרוּ	Qal, imperfect *waw*-consecutive, third-person, masculine, plural (אָמַר, to say)
אֵלָיו	preposition אֶל, with pronominal suffix (third-person, masculine, singular)
מַה	adverb, "what?"
נַּעֲשֶׂה	Qal, imperfect, first-person, common, plural (עָשָׂה, to do, make)
לָךְ	preposition לְ, with pronominal suffix (second-person, masculine, singular)
וְיִשְׁתֹּק	Qal, imperfect (jussive), third-person, masculine, singular (שָׁתַק, to be quiet, be silent)
הַיָּם	noun, masculine, singular, absolute (יָם, sea), with the definite article
מֵעָלֵינוּ	preposition עַל, with the preposition מִן, with pronominal suffix (first-person, common, plural)
כִּי	conjunction, "because"
הַיָּם	noun, masculine, singular, absolute (יָם, sea), with the definite article
הוֹלֵךְ	Qal, participle, active, masculine, singular, absolute (הָלַךְ, to go, walk)
וְסֹעֵר	Qal, participle, active, masculine, singular, absolute (סָעַר, to storm, rage)

Exegetical Notes:

1. The gentiles relentlessly question Jonah. This is now the seventh question that is posed to him. As God's prophet he should know the answers to their questions. What should they now do with Jonah because the situation has become even more urgent and dangerous?

2. Note the pausal form (indicating a clause break) of the preposition with the suffix, לָֽךְ. The form appears to be feminine, but it is masculine (לְךָ); the doubling of and the accent on the *lamedh* changes the *sewa* to a *qamets*. The pausal form of לָךְ occurs often in the Hebrew Bible, especially at the end of a sentence.

3. The preposition לְ may indicate advantage (meaning, "what may we do for you to help you?"), disadvantage (meaning, "what may we do against you to punish you?"), or it may simply be ambiguous (meaning, "what should we do in regard to you?").[41] The interpreter must make an exegetical decision on which meaning is to be preferred according to the context.

4. As before, the prepositional phrase מֵעָלֵינוּ ("from upon us") paints a picture of surrounding waves towering over them.

5. The causal clause כִּי הַיָּם הוֹלֵךְ וְסֹעֵר ("for the sea was becoming increasingly stormy") contains two participles that vividly portray the setting, lit. "the sea was continuously rushing and raging." The hendiadys communicates that the danger is changing from being threatening to being absolutely terrifying.[42] According to Chisholm, "The first participle is used adverbially; it indicates that the action described by the following verb was occurring continuously."[43] Snaith noted that the two participles are "idiomatic for 'getting rougher and rougher.'"[44]

---

41. Also, see Echols, *Reading Jonah*, 22.

42. Hendiadys (the term comes from Greek and means, "one through two") is another kind of literary device or figure of speech where the author uses two words linked with the conjunction "and" to express one idea (e.g., "silver and gold"). Hendiadys is used in literary texts for stylistic effect and emphasis.

43. Chisholm, *Workbook for Intermediate Hebrew*, 47.

44. Snaith, *Notes on the Hebrew Text of Jonah*, 19.

Jonah Flees

VERSE 12

Hebrew Text and Translation:

וַיֹּאמֶר אֲלֵיהֶם שָׂאוּנִי וַהֲטִילֻנִי אֶל־הַיָּם וְיִשְׁתֹּק הַיָּם מֵעֲלֵיכֶם כִּי יוֹדֵעַ אָנִי כִּי בְשֶׁלִּי הַסַּעַר הַגָּדוֹל הַזֶּה עֲלֵיכֶם:

And he said to them, "Pick me up and hurl me into the sea. Then the sea will become calm for (lit. from upon) you, for I know that on account of me this great storm *has come* upon you."

Grammatical Analysis:

וַיֹּאמֶר	Qal, imperfect *waw*-consecutive, third-person, masculine, singular (אָמַר, to say)
אֲלֵיהֶם	preposition אֶל, with pronominal suffix (third-person, masculine, plural)
שָׂאוּנִי	Qal, imperative, second-person, masculine, plural (נָשָׂא, to lift, carry, take), with verbal suffix (first-person, common, singular)
וַהֲטִילֻנִי	Hifil, imperative, second-person, masculine, plural (טוּל, to hurl, cast), with verbal suffix (first-person, common, singular), with conjunction
אֶל	preposition
הַיָּם	noun, masculine, singular, absolute (יָם, sea), with the definite article
וְיִשְׁתֹּק	Qal, imperfect (jussive), third-person, masculine, singular (שָׁתַק, to be quiet, be silent), with conjunction
הַיָּם	noun, masculine, singular, absolute (יָם, sea), with the definite article
מֵעֲלֵיכֶם	preposition עַל, with the preposition מִן, with pronominal suffix (second-person, masculine, plural)

The Book of Jonah

כִּי	conjunction, "because"
יוֹדֵעַ	Qal, participle, active, masculine singular, absolute (יָדַע, to know)
אָנִי	first personal pronoun, singular
כִּי	conjunction, "because" or "that"
בְשֶׁלִּי	relative pronoun שֶׁ, with preposition בְּ, with preposition לְ, with adverb pronominal suffix (first-person, common, singular)
הַסַּעַר	noun, masculine, singular, absolute (סַעַר, storm), with the definite article
הַגָּדוֹל	adjective, masculine, singular, absolute (גָּדוֹל, great), with the definite article
הַזֶּה	demonstrative pronoun זֶה (masculine, singular), with the definite article
עֲלֵיכֶם	preposition עַל, with pronominal suffix (second-person, masculine, plural)

Exegetical Notes:

1. Jonah's response again takes the reader by surprise. Instead of defending his actions as reasonable or obfuscating the main issue, he counsels the sailors to throw him overboard into the sea. Jonah is fearless and prepared to die for the sake of these gentiles. Yet, although Jonah knows that the Lord is pursuing him through the storm, he does not admit any guilt for wrongdoing.

2. Note the prepositional phrase מֵעֲלֵיכֶם ("from upon you"). It is as if the sea were attacking the ship with the sailors.

3. Here the first כִּי introduces a causal clause; as a prophet of God, Jonah knows the reason behind the storm. The second כִּי introduces the object clause of verbs of perception (such as knowing, thinking, saying, seeing, hearing, etc.); here we

Jonah Flees

translate "I know that on account of me this great storm *has come* upon you." Also note that we need to supply the verb in English in the last clause. The prepositional phrases, "on account of me" (בִּשְׁלִי) and "upon you" (עֲלֵיכֶם), are respectively placed at the beginning and the end of the sentence for emphasis. The sailors' lives are endangered by the presence of Jonah.

4. Verse 12 confirms the sailors' statement in verse 10 that Jonah had told them that the coming of the storm was on account of himself.

VERSE 13

Hebrew Text and Translation:

וַיַּחְתְּרוּ הָאֲנָשִׁים לְהָשִׁיב אֶל־הַיַּבָּשָׁה וְלֹא יָכֹלוּ
כִּי הַיָּם הוֹלֵךְ וְסֹעֵר עֲלֵיהֶם׃

Nevertheless, the men rowed to return to the dry land, but they could not (were not able to), for the sea was becoming *even* stormier against them (upon them).

Grammatical Analysis:

וַיַּחְתְּרוּ	Qal, imperfect *waw*-consecutive, third-person, masculine, plural (חָתַר, to dig, row)
הָאֲנָשִׁים	noun, masculine, plural, absolute (אִישׁ, man), with the definite article
לְהָשִׁיב	Hifil, infinitive, construct (שׁוּב, to turn, return)
אֶל	preposition
הַיַּבָּשָׁה	noun, feminine, singular, absolute (יַבָּשָׁה, dry land), with the definite article
וְלֹא	adverb "not," with the conjunction

יָכֹלוּ	Qal, perfect, third-person, common, plural (יָכֹל, to be able)
כִּי	conjunction, "because"
הַיָּם	noun, masculine, singular, absolute (יָם, sea), with the definite article
הוֹלֵךְ	Qal, participle, active, masculine, singular, absolute (הָלַךְ, to go, walk)
וְסֹעֵר	Qal, participle, active, masculine, singular, absolute (סָעַר, to storm, rage)
עֲלֵיהֶם	preposition, with pronominal suffix (third-person, masculine, plural)

Exegetical Notes:

1. The men's response reveals their noble character. Instead of immediately heeding Jonah's command to throw him into the sea, they still tried to preserve Jonah's life and reach safety through their efforts.

2. We may translate the imperfect *waw*-consecutive as "Nevertheless, the men continued to row to return the ship to the dry land." There is a contrast between Jonah's recommendation and the men's action. However, the men were not able to bring the ship to safety because of the ferocity of the storm.

3. Note the interesting use of the verb חָתַר, "to dig." The term is generally used to describe digging holes or digging through walls (for the purpose of burglary).[45] Here it is used for rowing since the action of rowing is like digging into the water. We note that the maritime vocabulary of the Hebrews, not being a seafaring people, was limited.

4. Again, note the use of אֲנָשִׁים, (men) instead of הַמַּלָּחִים (sailors). The term is an important word for the author and

---

45. In the ancient world, especially in the orient, homes were often constructed out of mudbrick. So, one could dig through a wall.

Jonah Flees

portrays the author's high regard for the sailors as human beings.

5. Note the return to the perfect tense יָכֹ֑לוּ ("but they could not"), indicating a circumstantial clause. The action of the verb occurred before or at the same time as the action of the preceding verb in the line of narration.

6. The expression כִּ֥י הַיָּ֖ם הוֹלֵ֥ךְ וְסֹעֵ֖ר עֲלֵיהֶֽם ("for the sea was becoming *even* stormier against them") is repeated, cf. verse 11. But here the prepositional phrase עֲלֵיהֶֽם ("upon them") is added for further intensification. We may translate the phrase as "against them."

VERSE 14

Hebrew Text and Translation:

וַיִּקְרְא֤וּ אֶל־יְהוָה֙ וַיֹּאמְר֔וּ
אָנָּ֤ה יְהוָה֙ אַל־נָ֣א נֹאבְדָ֗ה בְּנֶ֙פֶשׁ֙ הָאִ֣ישׁ הַזֶּ֔ה
וְאַל־תִּתֵּ֥ן עָלֵ֖ינוּ דָּ֣ם נָקִ֑יא
כִּֽי־אַתָּ֣ה יְהוָ֔ה כַּאֲשֶׁ֥ר חָפַ֖צְתָּ עָשִֽׂיתָ׃

Therefore, they called on the LORD and said, "O please, O LORD, may we please not perish on account of the life of this man and do not lay (impute) innocent blood on us; because You, O LORD, as You have planned, You did."

Grammatical Analysis:

וַיִּקְרְא֤וּ	Qal, imperfect *waw*-consecutive, third-person, masculine, plural (קָרָא, to call, proclaim, read)
אֶל	preposition
יְהוָה	proper name, "Yahweh," or conventionally "the LORD"
וַיֹּאמְר֔וּ	Qal, imperfect *waw*-consecutive, third-person, masculine, plural (אָמַר, to say)

The Book of Jonah

אָנָּה	particle of entreaty, or interjection "ah now!"
יְהוָה	proper name, "Yahweh," or conventionally "the LORD"
אַל	adverb, "not"
נָא	particle of entreaty, "please!"
נֹאבְדָה	Qal, imperfect (cohortative), first-person, common, plural (אָבַד, to perish)
בְּנֶפֶשׁ	noun, feminine, singular, absolute (נֶפֶשׁ, soul, life), with the preposition בְּ
הָאִישׁ	noun, masculine, singular, absolute (אִישׁ, man), with the definite article
הַזֶּה	demonstrative pronoun זֶה (masculine, singular), with the definite article
וְאַל	adverb, "not," with the conjunction
תִּתֵּן	Qal, imperfect (jussive), second-person, masculine, singular (נָתַן, to give, put)
עָלֵינוּ	preposition עַל, with pronominal suffix (first-person, common, plural)
דָּם	noun, masculine, singular, absolute (דָּם, blood)
נָקִיא	adjective, masculine, singular, absolute (נָקִיא, innocent)
כִּי	conjunction, "because"
אַתָּה	second personal pronoun, singular
יְהוָה	proper name, "Yahweh," or conventionally "the LORD"
כַּאֲשֶׁר	conjunction, "as," or "according to"
חָפַצְתָּ	Qal, perfect, second-person, masculine, singular (חָפֵץ, to delight in, plan)
עָשִׂיתָ	Qal, perfect, second-person, masculine, singular (עָשָׂה, to do, make)

Jonah Flees

Exegetical Notes:

1. Verse 14 is an important turning point or breakthrough in the story and the first recorded prayer. It continues to portray the innocence and humanity of the gentile sailors.

2. We may translate the conjunction *waw* as, "therefore." Jonah did not call on the LORD during the storm; instead the gentile sailors now invoke the mercy of the LORD.

3. The word אָנָּה ("oh please!") is a strong particle of entreaty. Under the threat of imminent death, people often use this term of desperation (2 Kgs 20:3; Isa 38:3; Ps 116:4,16; Dan 9:4; Neh 1:5, 11).

4. The cohortative in the prohibition also contains a particle of entreaty (נָא), "May we please not perish." The situation has become desperate for the sailors.

5. The prepositional phrase "on account of the life of this man" (בְּנֶפֶשׁ הָאִישׁ הַזֶּה) may either mean: 1) *"because* of the life of this man," or 2) *"with* the life of this man." In the first meaning, the sailors plead for forgiveness for what they are about to do. In the second meaning, the sailors plead that God will not punish them together with Jonah (that they may not perish with Jonah). The subsequent ceasing of the storm would later confirm to the sailors that Jonah was not innocent.

6. On the use of נֶפֶשׁ, Snaith observes, "Never translate נֶפֶשׁ, by 'soul.' No Hebrew ever had a 'soul.' He had a 'spirit.' The Greek had a 'soul,' and when Paul used the word, he referred to that which was 'natural' as against that which was 'spiritual.'"[46]

7. The following line also presents two possible interpretations: "And do not put on us (impute to us) innocent blood" (וְאַל־תִּתֵּן עָלֵינוּ דָּם נָקִיא). 1) The sailors pray that God would not punish them for killing an innocent man. They had no choice but were forced by circumstances to throw Jonah

---

46. Snaith, *Notes on the Hebrew Text of Jonah*, 21–22.

into the sea.⁴⁷ 2) Or the sailors pray that God will not punish them for killing an innocent man because Jonah was not innocent. They are acting as the instrument of divine justice and of the divine will by throwing Jonah into the sea. The reader must make an exegetical decision as to which meaning is preferred.

8. Note the use of synecdoche (a part of a thing is used to represent the whole thing). Jonah's blood represents his whole person or life. In the Old Testament, blood is often employed as a symbol referring to the life of a person (Gen 9:4–6; Lev 17:10–14; Ps 72:14).

9. The last line in the sailors' prayer reveals an important truth of salvation history (cf. Ps 115:3; 135:6). We may translate directly as "because You, O LORD, as You have planned, You did." The NASB has "for You, O LORD, have done as You have pleased." Some grammarians refer to the perfect here as a "confirmatory perfect," i.e., a perfect denoting an existing state. Wolff understood the perfect as a present with an iterative meaning, i.e., God always accomplishes what he has planned.

10. The verb חָפֵץ means "to delight in, to desire, to will, and to plan" and is significant in terms of our understanding of God's actions in history. God wills or plans what he delights in, and then he carries it out. The verb occurs eighty-six times in the Old Testament and often within the context of salvation history when God is the subject, especially as it concerns individuals or his anointed (cf. Ps 18:19; 22:8; 40:6, 8; 51:16, 19; 115:3; Isa 1:11; 42:21; 53:10–11; 62:4; Ezek 18:23, 32; 33:11; Mic 7:18). Likewise, in the book of Isaiah the cognate noun חֵפֶץ ("delight," "pleasure," "plan") frequently refers to God's plan of salvation (Isa 44:28; 46:10; 48:14; 53:10). The frequent use of key theological terms related to salvation history throughout the book of Jonah communicates to the reader that the events described in the book have typological significance.

---

47. There are many warnings in the Bible against the killing of innocent people (Deut 19:10, 13; 27:25; Prov 6:17).

Jonah Flees

VERSE 15

Hebrew Text and Translation:

וַיִּשְׂאוּ אֶת־יוֹנָה וַיְטִלֻהוּ אֶל־הַיָּם וַיַּעֲמֹד הַיָּם מִזַּעְפּוֹ׃

And so, they picked up Jonah, and hurled him into the sea, and consequently, the sea ceased from its rage.

Grammatical Analysis:

וַיִּשְׂאוּ	Qal, imperfect *waw*-consecutive, third-person, masculine, plural (נָשָׂא, to lift, carry, take)
אֶת	direct object marker
יוֹנָה	proper name, "Jonah" (alternative meaning, "dove")
וַיְטִלֻהוּ	Hifil, imperfect *waw*-consecutive, third-person, masculine, plural (טוּל, to hurl, cast), with verbal suffix (third-person, masculine, singular)
אֶל	preposition
הַיָּם	noun, masculine, singular, absolute (יָם, sea), with the definite article
וַיַּעֲמֹד	Qal, imperfect *waw*-consecutive, third-person, masculine, singular (עָמַד, to stand)
הַיָּם	noun, masculine, singular, absolute (יָם, sea), with the definite article
מִזַּעְפּוֹ	noun, masculine, singular, construct (זַעַף, storming, raging), with pronominal suffix (third-person, masculine, singular), and with the preposition מִן

The Book of Jonah

Exegetical Notes:

1. The looming crisis was averted when the sailors threw Jonah into the sea. Keil noted that "the sudden cessation of the storm showed that the bad weather had come entirely on Jonah's account, and that the sailors had not shed innocent blood by casting him into the sea."[48]

2. We may translate the imperfect *waw*-consecutive as "and so, they took Jonah . . ."

3. In verse 4, God hurled the storm upon the sea, which caused the sailors in verse 5 to hurl the cargo of the ship into the sea, and now finally they had no choice but to hurl Jonah into the sea.

4. We may translate the third imperfect *waw*-consecutive of the verse as "and consequently, the sea ceased from its raging."

5. Note the use of personification in terms of the sea ceasing to be angry. The verb עָמַד is often used for the calming down of anger (cf. 2 Chr 16:10; 26:19; Prov 19:12). Of course, in the context here it refers to the calming of God's anger against Jonah's disobeying the divine commission. In the context of the story, God's anger is graciously redirected now to focus on Jonah's preservation.

6. The word מִזַּעְפּוֹ (from זָעַף, to be enraged) is sometimes regarded as an infinitive construct with the third person masculine suffix and the preposition (cf. 2 Chr 26:19). Since an infinitive is a verbal noun, we may simply treat the word here as a noun (זַעַף, raging, or rage).

7. The storm began with God hurling a big wind upon the sea, and it ended with the sailors hurling Jonah into the sea. God's activity in nature compels the sailors to act in a certain way. God is in control but not in a fatalistic or mechanical way; there is true interaction between divine and human action.

---

48. Keil, *Twelve Minor Prophets*, 397.

8. Note the commentary on the sailors' experience in Ps 107:23–32. The sailors are among the groups of people who are obligated to praise God for his loving-kindness. They are even welcomed within the assembly of the elders to extol God's wonderful works. The psalmist applies experiences from ordinary life to represent Israel's experience in salvation history.

VERSE 16

Hebrew Text and Translation:

וַיִּֽירְא֧וּ הָאֲנָשִׁ֛ים יִרְאָ֥ה גְדוֹלָ֖ה אֶת־יְהוָ֑ה
וַיִּֽזְבְּחוּ־זֶ֙בַח֙ לַֽיהוָ֔ה וַֽיִּדְּר֖וּ נְדָרִֽים׃

As a result, the men feared the LORD with a great fear, and they offered a sacrifice to the LORD and made vows.

Grammatical Analysis:

וַיִּֽירְאוּ	Qal, imperfect *waw*-consecutive, third-person, masculine, plural (יָרֵא, to fear)
הָאֲנָשִׁים	noun, masculine, plural, absolute (אִישׁ, man), with the definite article
יִרְאָה	noun, feminine, singular, absolute (יִרְאָה, fear)
גְדוֹלָה	adjective, feminine, singular, absolute (גָּדוֹל, great)
אֶת	direct object marker
יְהוָה	proper name, "Yahweh," or conventionally "the LORD"
וַיִּזְבְּחוּ	Qal, imperfect *waw*-consecutive, third-person, masculine, plural (זָבַח, to slaughter, sacrifice)
זֶבַח	noun, masculine, singular, absolute (זֶבַח, sacrifice)
לַיהוָה	proper name, "Yahweh," or conventionally "the LORD," with preposition לְ

| וַיִּדְּרוּ | Qal, imperfect *waw*-consecutive, third-person, masculine, plural (נָדַר, to vow) |
| נְדָרִים | noun, masculine, plural, absolute (נֶדֶר, vow) |

Exegetical Notes:

1. Verse 16 does not relate anything about Jonah to the reader, but the author nevertheless includes the statement concerning the sailors' response to their experience. It underscores the importance of the gentiles for the author.

2. We may translate the imperfect *waw*-consecutive as follows, "As a result, the men feared the LORD with a great fear . . ." Note the use of the cognate accusative.

3. The addition of the phrase אֶת־יְהוָה ("Yahweh") is important (cf. verse 10).[49] Some commentators regard the phrase as a later insertion into the text; however there is no textual evidence for it. The Hebrew Bible often uses the generic term "God" (אֱלֹהִים) when it talks about God in general but uses the LORD (יְהוָה) when a personal covenant relationship is in view. We may conclude that the men gained a true knowledge of God and became true worshipers of the LORD.

4. Observe the development in the sailors' knowledge of God. In verse 5 they feared, then in verse 10 they feared greatly, and finally in verse 16 they feared the LORD. In Deuteronomy one of the main injunctions upon the Israelites in terms of covenant faithfulness is to fear the LORD (cf. Deut 10:12). This injunction to fear the LORD should not be understood as an injunction to be terrified of the LORD but as one that calls for reverence and devotion.

5. The interpretation or translation given in the *UBS Translation Handbook* is quite inaccurate: "This made the sailors so

---

49. The direct object marker often stands before proper nouns.

afraid of the LORD that they offered a sacrifice and promised to serve him."⁵⁰

6. The verb זָבַח (to slaughter, to sacrifice) can be used for a thanksgiving offering (cf. Lev 7:12; Ps 107:22).

7. The vows the men made indicate that they became perpetual worshipers of the LORD.

---

50. Clark, *Handbook on the Books of Obadiah, Jonah, and Micah*, 70–71.

2

Jonah Prays

VERSE 1

Hebrew Text and Translation:

וַיְמַן יְהוָה דָּג גָּדוֹל לִבְלֹעַ אֶת־יוֹנָה
וַיְהִי יוֹנָה בִּמְעֵי הַדָּג שְׁלֹשָׁה יָמִים וּשְׁלֹשָׁה לֵילוֹת׃

And the LORD appointed a great fish to swallow Jonah. And it came to pass that Jonah was in the bowels of the fish three days and three nights.

Grammatical Analysis:

וַיְמַן	Piel, imperfect *waw*-consecutive, third-person, masculine, singular (מָנָה, to appoint, assign)
יְהוָה	proper name, "Yahweh," or conventionally "the LORD"
דָּג	noun, masculine, singular, absolute (דָּג, fish)
גָּדוֹל	adjective, masculine, singular, absolute (גָּדוֹל, great)
לִבְלֹעַ	Qal, infinitive, construct (בָּלַע, to swallow)

Jonah Prays

אֶת	direct object marker
יוֹנָה	proper name, "Jonah" (alternative meaning, "dove")
וַיְהִי	Qal, imperfect *waw*-consecutive, third-person, masculine, singular (הָיָה, to be, become, is)
יוֹנָה	proper name, "Jonah" (alternative meaning, "dove")
בִּמְעֵי	noun, masculine, plural, construct (מֵעֶה, inward parts, bowels), with the preposition בְּ
הַדָּג	noun, masculine, singular, absolute (דָּג, fish), with definite article
שְׁלֹשָׁה	noun, feminine, singular, absolute (שָׁלֹשׁ, three)
יָמִים	noun, masculine, plural, absolute (יוֹם, day)
וּשְׁלֹשָׁה	noun, feminine, singular, absolute (שָׁלֹשׁ, three), with conjunction
לֵילוֹת	noun, masculine, plural, absolute (לַיְלָה, night)

Exegetical Notes:

1. The verb מָנָה occurs four times in the book of Jonah and always describes the Lord's intervention in nature and history (Jonah 2:1; 4:6,7,8). The verb also occurs in the book of Daniel where the Babylonian king appointed overseers and food for the Jewish exiles (Dan 1:5, 10–11). This Babylonian context is significant for interpreting the book of Jonah. God uses extraordinary means to preserve his people. In Ps 61:8 (verse 7 in the English versions) God appoints loving-kindness and faithfulness for the preservation of his people. The verb is also used in Isa 53:12, where the righteous servant was "numbered (or appointed) with the transgressors."

2. The fish, occurring four times in chapter 2, is the instrument of divine deliverance (Jonah 2:1, 2, 11).

3. The last line of verse 1 is a summary statement; the subsequent verses explain what happened in detail. Often in

Hebrew narrative a summary statement is given at the beginning of the narrative (e.g., Gen 1:1; 37:5; Dan 1:9; 9:24). Here prose narrative is followed by poetry (a psalm).

4. With respect to the expression שְׁלֹשָׁה יָמִים וּשְׁלֹשָׁה לֵילוֹת, note the rules for Hebrew numerals. Numbers from three to ten function as collectives (therefore singular) and differ in gender (feminine numerals are used with masculine nouns). When the noun is anarthrous, the numeral precedes the noun.[1]

5. The expression "three days and three nights" also requires explanation. Time references to "three days and three nights," "three days," and the "third day" occur several times in the Old Testament and refer to a period of time spanning three days.[2] These expressions do not necessarily encompass a literal seventy-two-hour period with three whole nights and three whole days.[3] It was a common practice in early Judaism to count a part of a day as a whole day.[4] Therefore, Jesus' reference to Jonah in Matt 12:39–40 should not be understood literally but as an idiom indicating a period encompassing three days (cf. Matt 17:23; 20:19; 27:64). Jesus was crucified on Friday and rose from the dead Sunday morning at or before daybreak, encompassing a time span of three days.

---

1. Also see Ferreira, *Old Testament Hebrew*, 48.

2. See Gen 30:36; 40:12–13, 18–19; Exod 3:18; 5:3; 10:22; 15:22; 19:9–11; Num 10:33; 33:8; Josh 1:11; 2:16, 22; 3:2; Judg 14:14; 19:4; 1 Sam 9:20; 30:12–13; 1 Kgs 12:5; 2 Kgs 2:17; 1 Chr 12:39; 2 Chr 10:5; Ezra 8:15, 32; 10:8–9; Neh 2:11; Esth 4:16; Hos 6:2.

3. The reader's attention is especially drawn to Exod 19:9–11, 1 Sam 30:11–13, and Esth 4:16—5:1.

4. For example, see *Jerusalem Talmud*: Shabbath ix. 3.

Jonah Prays

VERSE 2

Hebrew Text and Translation:

וַיִּתְפַּלֵּל יוֹנָה אֶל־יְהוָה אֱלֹהָיו מִמְּעֵי הַדָּגָה:

Then Jonah prayed to the LORD his God from the bowels of the fish,

Grammatical Analysis:

וַיִּתְפַּלֵּל	Hithpael, imperfect *waw*-consecutive, third-person, masculine, singular (פָּלַל, to intervene, pray)
יוֹנָה	proper name, "Jonah" (alternative meaning, "dove")
אֶל	preposition
יְהוָה	proper name, "Yahweh," or conventionally "the LORD"
אֱלֹהָיו	noun, masculine, plural, construct (אֱלֹהִים, God, gods), with pronominal suffix (third-person, masculine, singular)
מִמְּעֵי	noun, masculine, plural, construct (מֵעֶה, inward parts, bowels), with preposition מִן
הַדָּגָה	noun, feminine, singular, absolute (דָּג, fish), with definite article

Exegetical Notes:

1. The stem פָּלַל is frequently used in the Hithpael for prayer. The basic meaning of the root is "to intervene." Prayer is often a request for God to intervene in history for the salvation of his people. In the Piel the verb means "to judge." The idea behind the biblical notion of prayer is for God to intervene in human affairs in order to establish righteousness and justice on the earth.

2. The expression "his God" (אֱלֹהָיו) is in apposition to "the LORD" (יְהוָה). It is interesting to note that while Jonah is disobedient and while he has misgivings about God, the author still refers to the LORD as being "his God." Despite Jonah's disobedience, God does not abandon his prophet.

3. Note that "fish" in verse 1 is the masculine form (הַדָּג), but here it is the feminine form (הַדָּגָה). No satisfactory solution has been offered to explain the change from the masculine noun in verse 1 to the feminine noun in verse 2. The masculine form occurs nineteen times in the Old Testament, and except for Num 13:16 and the occurrences in Jonah, it is always plural. The feminine occurs thirteen times and is always used in the singular as a collective noun. Perhaps, the choice of the feminine in verse 2 suggests a link with the creation account where God granted man dominion over the fish (feminine, singular) of the sea (Gen 1:26, 28). Jonah, instead of having dominion over the works of the LORD's hands, is subjugated by sea creatures (his subjects) due to his disobedience (cf. Ps 8). There is an inversion of the creation order. The Septuagint renders the noun as "sea monster" (κῆτος), which is neuter in verse 1 as well as in verse 2.

4. Another explanation for the change from the masculine to the feminine could be that verses 2 to 10, containing the psalm with its introduction, was composed at a later date and inserted into the prose narrative of the book. In terms of the flow of the narrative, there is no disjunction between verses 1 and 11. The psalm forms a distinct unit which describes Jonah's experience in more general terms, hence the term for fish in verse 3 uses the generic term for fish (feminine) rather than pointing to the particular big fish (masculine) that swallowed Jonah.[5]

---

5. Since we believe that inspiration goes down to every letter of the text (Matt 5:18), it is important to reflect on these details. A credible explanation may escape us for the moment, but every detail of the Hebrew text is significant.

Jonah Prays

VERSE 3

Hebrew Text and Translation:

וַיֹּאמֶר קָרָאתִי מִצָּרָה לִי אֶל־יְהוָה וַיַּעֲנֵנִי
מִבֶּטֶן שְׁאוֹל שִׁוַּעְתִּי שָׁמַעְתָּ קוֹלִי:

> saying,
> "I called from my distress to the LORD,
> and He answered me;
> from the womb of Sheol I cried out,
> and You heard my voice.

Grammatical Analysis:

וַיֹּאמֶר	Qal, imperfect *waw*-consecutive, third-person, masculine, singular (אָמַר, to say)
קָרָאתִי	Qal, perfect, first-person, common, singular (קָרָא, to cry out, call)
מִצָּרָה	noun, feminine, singular, absolute (צָרָה, distress), with preposition מִן
לִי	preposition, with pronominal suffix (first-person, singular, common)
אֶל	preposition
יְהוָה	proper name, "Yahweh," or conventionally "the LORD"
וַיַּעֲנֵנִי	Qal, imperfect *waw*-consecutive, third-person, masculine, singular (עָנָה, to answer), with pronominal object (first-person, common, singular)
מִבֶּטֶן	noun, feminine, singular, construct (בֶּטֶן, belly, body, womb), with preposition מִן
שְׁאוֹל	noun, masculine, singular, absolute (שְׁאוֹל, place of the dead, grave, hell)

שִׁוַּעְתִּי	Piel, perfect, first-person, common, singular (שָׁוַע, to cry out)
שָׁמָעְתָּ	Qal, perfect, second-person, masculine, singular (שָׁמַע, to hear)
קוֹלִי	noun, masculine, singular, construct (קוֹל, sound, voice)

Exegetical Notes:

1. Jonah finally calls upon God. Jonah's prayer from the inner parts of the fish and Jonah's glorious deliverance from tribulation encourage God's people to call upon him whenever life is very dark. The Christian is never without hope. The prophet Jeremiah may well have reflected on the story of Jonah as an encouragement to pray during the exilic experience (cf. Jer 51:34). Jonah, as a representative of Israel, may be a symbolic portrayal of Israel's experience in exile. So, Snaith comments, "The prayer of Jonah from the belly of the fish is the prayer of exiled Israel; cf. Jeremiah 51:34."[6]

2. Much as we sometimes have in narrative, the first line of the psalm provides the theme or the summary of the whole psalm. The following verses provide the details. The psalm in chapter 2 was composed after Jonah experienced the distress and deliverance from the bowels of the fish. It is a psalm of thanksgiving for deliverance, and it was written after the event.[7] Obviously, Jonah would not be writing a psalm in the bowels of a fish.

3. In verse 3, the first verse of the psalm, the author employs synonymous parallelism to express his sentiment. But remember that in synonymous parallelism, the second line adds something new to the meaning of the first line (see discussion below).

---

6. Snaith, *Notes on the Hebrew Text of Jonah*, 24.

7. We disagree with Echols, who regards the psalm as a lament. See Echols, *Reading Jonah*, 33–34.

Jonah Prays

4. Note the Qinah metre (3:2 stress pattern in each line), which is often used in lament. In order to complete the stress pattern, the preposition with the pronominal suffix is used (לִי) instead of simply the pronominal suffix attached to the noun.

5. Also note the assonance in the frequent use of the pronominal suffix—î (ִי); the assonance puts the emphasis on Jonah or serves to highlight Jonah's experience of deliverance.

6. It is important to observe that a different word (בֶּטֶן) is used in the expression "womb of Sheol" than the word (מֵעֶה) in the expression "bowels of the fish" in the previous verses (some versions do not make this distinction). The previous verses describe Jonah's situation physically, while the psalm describes his situation spiritually. Although the terms appear in synonymous construction (Gen 25:23; Num 5:22; Ps 71:6), strictly speaking מֵעֶה never means "womb" since it is always in the plural form. The word בֶּטֶן often refers to the womb, the organ that gives birth to new life (Gen 25:24; Deut 7:13; Ps 22:9–10; 139:13; Isa 44:2,24; 49:1). As such, according to particular contexts, it is a positive term that designates the beginning of new life. Although Jonah finds himself in the midst of great turmoil, his experience gives birth to a new beginning. In other words, the meaning of the first line is amplified in the second.

7. We need to make a comment on the Hebrew term Sheol (שְׁאוֹל). The term occurs sixty-five times in the Old Testament. The term generally refers to the place of the dead or the place of departed souls (the underworld); it refers to the place where people go after they die. Therefore, often it may simply be translated as "the grave" (Gen 37:35; 42:38; 44:29). However, many scriptural passages indicate that the destination of the wicked is different from the destination of the righteous. Death comes upon the wicked and they go down into Sheol; their freedom is taken away and they are punished (Num 16:30, 33; Deut 32:22; Ps 9:17; 55:15). Sheol can thus be a place of distress and torment (Ps 18:5–6; 116:3; Prov

15:11), and so, many translations sometimes render the term as "hell."[8] In the New Testament, the theology of heaven and hell becomes much more distinct. In a way, Sheol in the Old Testament, the place where all the dead go, becomes more specific as either heaven or hell in the New Testament. From a New Testament perspective Sheol covers both heaven and hell.[9] But since death is the result of sin and the ideal life is bodily existence (Gen 2:7), Sheol often carries a negative connotation in the Old Testament.

8. Note the perfect tense of the last two verbs in the verse, שִׁוַּעְתִּי ("I cried out") and שָׁמַעְתָּ ("you heard"). If we follow the normal function of the tenses in narrative, the second line provides a further or a deeper explanation of the first line. The answer from the womb of Sheol preceded the answer from the distress in the bowels of the fish. Also note that the first line is rendered in the third person ("He answered me"), whereas the second line in the second person ("You heard my voice"). The second line is more intimate than the first.[10] Therefore, Jonah's rescue from the fish is not just something physical; it is profoundly spiritual. The LORD not only answered Jonah's cry from his distress but also from the womb of Sheol. Spiritual deliverance preceded physical deliverance, or the basis of Jonah's physical deliverance (being vomited out on dry land) was spiritual deliverance.[11]

---

8. Chisholm's criticism of the KJV's "hell" as being "misleading" is too severe. The meaning of words depends on their contexts and often requires interpretation. See Chisholm, *Workbook for Intermediate Hebrew*, 57.

9. We note here the idea of progressive revelation. God's truth becomes clearer as salvation history unfolds.

10. Also note the comment by Echols: "In line A Jonah addresses YHWH in the third-person, but in B² he shifts to the second-person. The change has the effect of heightening the sense of spiritual intimacy or proximity between YHWH and Jonah." See Echols, *Reading Jonah*, 35.

11. In the Old Testament, after the fall, spiritual condemnation preceded physical death (Gen 3:19). We note the same order with respect to ultimate punishment and ultimate salvation in the New Testament; spiritual death precedes bodily condemnation, and spiritual resurrection precedes bodily resurrection (cf. Rev 20).

Jonah Prays

VERSE 4

Hebrew Text and Translation:

וַתַּשְׁלִיכֵ֤נִי מְצוּלָה֙ בִּלְבַ֣ב יַמִּ֔ים וְנָהָ֖ר יְסֹבְבֵ֑נִי
כָּל־מִשְׁבָּרֶ֥יךָ וְגַלֶּ֖יךָ עָלַ֥י עָבָֽרוּ׃

For You threw me into the depth,
into the heart of the seas,
and a flood incessantly surrounded me;
all Your breakers and Your waves
had passed over me.

Grammatical Analysis:

וַתַּשְׁלִיכֵ֤נִי	Hifil, imperfect *waw*-consecutive, second-person, masculine, singular (שָׁלַךְ, to throw), with verbal pronominal suffix (first-person, common, singular)
מְצוּלָה	noun, feminine, singular, absolute (מְצוֹלָה, depth, deep)
בִּלְבַב	noun, masculine, singular, construct (לֵבָב, heart)
יַמִּים	noun, masculine, plural, absolute (יָם, sea)
וְנָהָר	noun, masculine, singular, absolute (נָהָר, stream, river)
יְסֹבְבֵנִי	Piel, imperfect, third-person, masculine, singular (סָבַב, to surround, go around), with verbal pronominal suffix (first-person, common, singular)
כָּל	noun, masculine, singular, construct (כֹּל, the whole, all)
מִשְׁבָּרֶיךָ	noun, masculine, plural, construct (מִשְׁבָּר, breaker), with pronominal suffix (second-person masculine singular)
וְגַלֶּיךָ	noun, masculine, plural, construct (גַּל, wave, billow)
עָלַי	preposition, with pronominal suffix (first-person, common, singular)

עָבָרוּ   Qal, perfect, third-person, masculine, plural (עָבַר, to pass over)

Exegetical Notes:

1. Verses 4 to 7a describe the severity of Jonah's condition and torment.

2. Although according to chapter 1, the sailors threw Jonah into the sea, Jonah correctly interprets their action as God's action. Note the Hifil stem, which implies, "You caused me to be thrown into the depth." Jonah attributed the reason for his humiliation to God.

3. Notice that in the first line, with the addition of the word מְצוּלָה ("depth" or "deep"), the stress pattern is broken. Instead of a 3:2, we have a 4:2 metre. The broken pattern increases the feeling of anxiety and indicates the chaos of Jonah's situation. Some scholars prefer to omit the word מְצוּלָה to maintain a consistent rhythm.[12] However, since there is no manuscript evidence that this word was added later, we would argue that the extra word was intentionally added by the author to indicate the chaotic nature of Jonah's predicament. Also note that we translated the term as "depth" since we will translate תְהוֹם in verse 6 as "the deep."

4. The term מְצוּלָה ("deep") is often used as a metaphor of distress (cf. Ps 68:22; 69:3,15; 88:7).

5. Observe that the subject in the second line נָהָר is placed before the verb for emphasis. The word refers to a "river" or a "flood" which has a permanent flow of water as opposed to a "wadi" (נַחַל), which is mostly dry. Although the article often drops out in poetry, there is no need to translate the noun with a definite article since no particular flood is in view here. Some translations translate "river" as a "current" because the context refers to the sea; however, one does not

---

12. See Snaith, *Notes on the Hebrew Text of Jonah*, 25.

Jonah Prays

need to be overly exact in the use of oceanographic terms in poetry. Since the term "current" does not carry the symbolic association with judgment as "flood" does, we still prefer the term "flood."

6. The tense of the verb סָבַב (to surround) is in the imperfect. The imperfect may be used in poetry to denote frequentative action (the so-called frequentative imperfect). In the context here it is used to describe the psalmist's past experience.

7. As the last verbs in the previous verse, the last verb is in the perfect tense (עָבָרוּ), indicating action at the same time or action preceding the action of the previous verb in the line of narration (וַתְּשַׁלִיכֵנִי). The use of the Hebrew tenses reflects the physical sequence of being thrown into the depths of the sea; one would first experience the waves of the sea on the surface before one would sink to the bottom of the ocean.

8. The use of floods, waves and billows as a picture of turmoil and judgment are often found in poetry (cf. Job 27:20; Ps 18:4; 42:7; 69:2; 88:7). Noah's flood and the destruction of the Egyptians in the Reed Sea naturally lead to the use of water as a symbol of God's judgment.

9. We may make a final theological point here. Strictly speaking, Jonah's statement, "all Your breakers and Your waves had passed over me," is not correct. "Breakers" and "waves" are metaphors of God's judgment. To use the noun all (כָּל), which means "totality,"[13] in relation to God's judgment is an execration or hyperbole. If the full force or totality of God's judgment were unleashed upon Jonah, he would not have been able to bear it. Or perhaps a better interpretation is that Jonah here is going beyond his own experience and is talking about another. The totality of God's judgment upon rebellion and sin was only unleashed upon the Lord Jesus when he was crucified on the cross.

---

13. The noun is usually translated as an adjective ("all") in English.

10. We may understand the parallelism here as synthetic. The second and third line of the verse develop the idea expressed in the first line.

VERSE 5

Hebrew Text and Translation:

וַאֲנִי אָמַרְתִּי נִגְרַשְׁתִּי מִנֶּגֶד עֵינֶיךָ
אַךְ אוֹסִיף לְהַבִּיט אֶל־הֵיכַל קָדְשֶׁךָ:

But I said, "I have been driven away from before Your eyes; yet I shall again look upon Your holy temple.

Grammatical Analysis:

וַאֲנִי	first personal pronoun, singular, with the conjunction
אָמַרְתִּי	Qal, perfect, first-person, common, singular (אָמַר, to say)
נִגְרַשְׁתִּי	Nifal, perfect, first-person, common, singular (גָּרַשׁ, to drive out, cast out)
מִנֶּגֶד	preposition נֶגֶד ("in front," "before"), with preposition מִן
עֵינֶיךָ	noun, masculine, dual, construct (עַיִן, eye), with pronominal suffix (second-person, masculine, singular)
אַךְ	adverb, "surely," "indeed"
אוֹסִיף	Hifil, imperfect *waw*-consecutive, 1st common, singular (יָסַף, to add, do again)
לְהַבִּיט	Hifil, infinitive, construct (נָבַט, to look)
אֶל	preposition
הֵיכַל	noun, masculine, singular, construct (הֵיכָל, palace, temple)

Jonah Prays

קָדְשֶׁךָ   noun, masculine, singular, construct (קֹדֶשׁ, holiness), with pronominal suffix (second-person, masculine, singular)

Exegetical Notes:

1. The first conjunction *waw* provides a contrast with the preceding verse in light of Jonah's expression of faith, "yet I shall again look upon Your holy temple," so we translate it as "but."

2. Note the addition of the personal pronoun אֲנִי to maintain the metre as well as to emphasize the grievance of the psalmist. The pronoun is placed before the verb for emphasis.

3. Note the use of the perfect tense אָמַרְתִּי ("I have said"). The psalmist's reflection or prayer here happened while he was experiencing the turmoil of the previous verse. It functions as a flashback.

4. The Nifal of the verb נִגְרַשְׁתִּי may either be a passive or a reflexive, "I have been driven away from before Your eyes," or "I have removed myself from Your eyes." Also note the use of the perfect tense.

5. It is important to point out that the verb גָּרַשׁ (to drive out) is also used in Gen 3:24 (also cf. Gen 4:14), where Adam and Eve are expelled from the garden of Eden. This is another hint that the prophetic text goes beyond the personal experience of Jonah and relates to the events of salvation history. The verb is used to describe broken relationships such as a divorce (Lev 21:7,14; 22:13; Num 30:9; Hos 9:15).

6. According to Snaith, the particle אַךְ "always involves something contrary to what has been said or is expected."[14] One would expect that Jonah would have lost all hope in his current situation, yet he still believed that he would be saved.

---

14. Snaith, *Notes on the Hebrew Text of Jonah*, 26.

7. Jonah not only believes that he will be rescued but also that he will again experience the presence of the LORD in the temple. Although Jonah is from Northern Israel, he still regards the temple in Jerusalem as the legitimate dwelling place of the LORD. The expression "הֵיכַל קָדְשֶׁךָ" often occurs in the book of Psalms; it is only because of God's mercy (חֶסֶד) that the psalmist gains access to the temple (cf. Ps 5:7; 11:4; 65:4; 138:2).

8. It is also interesting to observe that the regular stress pattern or metre of the poetry is now restored (3:2). With faith, order and calm return to Jonah's mood.

9. Finally, note the antithetic parallelism. Being "driven away" is contrasted with "I shall again look upon Your holy temple."

VERSE 6

Hebrew Text and Translation:

אֲפָפוּנִי מַיִם עַד־נֶפֶשׁ תְּהוֹם יְסֹבְבֵנִי
סוּף חָבוּשׁ לְרֹאשִׁי לְקִצְבֵי הָרִים׃

The waters encompassed me, against my soul;
the deep constantly surrounded me;
reeds were wrapped about my head,
to the roots of the mountains.

Grammatical Analysis:

אֲפָפוּנִי	Qal, perfect *waw*-consecutive, third-person, masculine, plural (אָפַף, to surround, encompass), with verbal pronominal suffix (first-person, common, singular)
מַיִם	noun, masculine, plural, absolute (מַיִם, water)
עַד	preposition
נֶפֶשׁ	noun, feminine, singular, absolute (נֶפֶשׁ, soul, life)

Jonah Prays

תְּהוֹם	noun, masculine, singular, absolute (תְּהוֹם, deep, abyss)
יְסֹבְבֵנִי	Piel, imperfect, third-person, masculine, plural (סָבַב, to turn around, surround), with verbal pronominal suffix (first-person, common, singular)
סוּף	noun, masculine, singular, absolute (סוּף, reeds, rushes)
חָבוּשׁ	Qal, participle passive, masculine, singular, absolute (חָבַשׁ, to bind)
לְרֹאשִׁי	noun, masculine, singular, construct (רֹאשׁ, head), with pronominal suffix (first-person, common, singular), with preposition לְ
לְקִצְבֵי	noun, masculine, plural, construct (קֶצֶב, extremity, end), with preposition לְ
הָרִים	noun, masculine, plural, absolute (הַר, mountain)

Exegetical Notes:

1. Verse 6 (synonymous parallelism) continues to describe the predicament of the psalmist.

2. The preposition עַד (as far as, even to, up to, until) is used in terms of degree "to the extent of," and in the context implies opposition or hostility. We have translated נֶפֶשׁ as "soul" to indicate the spiritual nature of Jonah's turmoil. Also, note the *zaqeph qaton* (˙) above the letter *nun* to indicate a sense division in the text.

3. In the second line, the subject תְּהוֹם is placed before the verb for emphasis. We translated the term with the article since "the deep" refers to extreme forces of turmoil and even darkness that God brings to bear upon the world (cf. Gen 1:2; 7:11; Isa 45:7). The article is often omitted in poetry. Snaith comments, "תהום is not the ordinary ocean, but the vasty primeval Deep, personified in the Babylonian Tiamat (equals the Hebrew Tehom), or the Hebrew Rahab."[15]

15. Snaith, *Notes on the Hebrew Text of Jonah*, 27.

4. Note the use of the imperfect יְסֹבְבֵנִי to indicate frequentative action. The *ethnak* underneath the letter *beth* indicates the major verse division.

5. The term סוּף is a collective noun, so we may translate it with the plural in English as "reeds." It is also interesting to note here that it was through the Sea of Reeds (יַם־סוּף) that God saved the Israelites from the Egyptians. Here is another linking of Jonah's experience with the events of salvation history. In the book of Exodus, the Reed Sea meant judgment for the Egyptians but salvation for the Israelites. In the same way, the sea and the fish in the book of Jonah are instruments of judgment as well as of salvation. So too, the cross of the Lord Jesus is a symbol of judgment as well as of salvation.

6. The preposition לְ here indicates the direct object of the verb.[16]

7. Note the different verse division here. We follow the suggestion of Snaith and Wolff by attaching the phrase לְקִצְבֵי הָרִים to the last line of verse 6 in order to maintain the stress pattern.[17] The Septuagint also connects the expression with the content of verse 6 (ἔδυ ἡ κεφαλή μου εἰς σχισμὰς ὀρέων). The full meaning or theological significance of the expression "to the roots of the mountains" still escapes our understanding.

VERSE 7

Hebrew Text and Translation:

יָרַדְתִּי הָאָרֶץ בְּרִחֶיהָ בַעֲדִי לְעוֹלָם וַתַּעַל מִשַּׁחַת חַיַּי יְהוָה אֱלֹהָי:

> I went down into the earth,
> its bars *tried to shut* me in forever.
> Yet, You brought up my life from the pit,
> O Lord, my God.

16. Ferreira, *Old Testament Hebrew*, 27.

17. The editors of the *Biblia Hebraica Stuttgartensia* also assigned the expression to the last line of verse 6.

Jonah Prays

Grammatical Analysis:

יָרַדְתִּי	Qal, perfect, first-person, common, singular (יָרַד, to go down, to descend)
הָאָרֶץ	noun, feminine, singular, absolute (אֶרֶץ, earth, land), with the definite article
בְּרִחֶיהָ	noun, masculine, plural, construct (בְּרִיחַ, bar), with pronominal suffix (third-person, feminine, singular)
בַעֲדִי	preposition (בַּעַד, away from, behind, about, upon, on behalf of)
לְעוֹלָם	noun, masculine, singular, absolute (עוֹלָם, forever), with preposition לְ
וַתַּעַל	Hifil, imperfect *waw*-consecutive, second-person, masculine, singular, opposite of יָרַד (עָלָה, to go up, ascend)
מִשַּׁחַת	noun, feminine, singular, absolute (שַׁחַת, pit), with preposition מִן
חַיַּי	noun, masculine, plural, construct (חַי, life), with pronominal suffix (first-person, common, singular)
יְהוָה	proper name, "Yahweh," or conventionally "the LORD"
אֱלֹהָי	noun, masculine, plural, construct (אֱלֹהִים, God, gods), with pronominal suffix (third-person, masculine, singular), with pronominal suffix (first-person, common, singular)

Exegetical Notes:

1. The term בְּרִיחַ is figuratively used of distress (Ps 107:16; Prov 18:19).
2. The preposition בַּעַד means "behind" or "round about." It is used with verbs of shutting, in the sense of to shut behind, i.e., to shut one in (Judg 3:23; 2 Kgs 4:4,5,33; Isa 26:20). In the

context of the line, one must supply the verb. Since Jonah was rescued, we insert a conative verb.[18]

3. In the second line of the verse, the lament turns into thanksgiving. Since there is a contrast between the first and second line of the verse, we translate the *waw* as an adversative conjunction, "yet" or "but."

4. The form of verbs which are both pe-guttural (initial guttural verbs) and lamedh-he (final ה verbs) are the same in the Qal and Hifil stems. In such instances one has to rely on the context to make the distinction. Here the verb is Hifil because it is transitive.

5. The term שַׁחַת ("pit") is often used in the Psalms to refer to a trap (Ps 7:16; 35:7) and may also describe a state of helplessness, corruption, and destruction (Ps 16:10; 30:10; 49:10; 55:24; Job 33:24). It is also used synonymously or in parallel construction with Sheol (Ps 16:10; Prov 1:12; Isa 14:15; 38:18). One may recall the story of Joseph, who was cast into a well. The hapless lad had no way of escape but had to rely on Reuben for deliverance.

6. Note again that the article is often omitted in poetry, so we may translate מִשַּׁחַת as "from the pit."

7. It is important to observe that the verb עָלָה (to go up) is often used in connection with deliverance from Egypt (cf. Exod 13:38; 33:1; Deut 1:21) and personal or individual deliverance from death (cf. Ps 30:3; 71:20; 103:4). In other words, there is another link here with Israel's experience in salvation history.

8. After "my life," the Dead Sea Scroll text adds "my soul" (נפשי) (4Q82 Minor Prophets).

9. The last two words of the line may either be translated as a vocative ("O LORD, my God) or as a noun sentence ("Yahweh is my God"). In the context, the vocative is to be preferred.

---

18. Conative in grammar refers to an attempted action.

Jonah Prays

VERSE 8

Hebrew Text and Translation:

בְּהִתְעַטֵּף עָלַי נַפְשִׁי אֶת־יְהוָה זָכָרְתִּי
וַתָּבוֹא אֵלֶיךָ תְּפִלָּתִי אֶל־הֵיכַל קָדְשֶׁךָ׃

When my life was fainting away,
I remembered the LORD,
and my prayer came to You,
into Your holy temple.

Grammatical Analysis:

בְּהִתְעַטֵּף	Hithpael, infinitive, construct (עָטַף, to be feeble, faint), with preposition בְּ
עָלַי	preposition, with pronominal suffix (first-person, common, singular)
נַפְשִׁי	noun, feminine, singular, absolute (נֶפֶשׁ, soul, life), with pronominal suffix (first-person, common, singular)
אֶת	direct object marker
יְהוָה	proper name, "Yahweh," or conventionally "the LORD"
זָכָרְתִּי	Qal, perfect, first-person, common, singular (זָכַר, to remember)
וַתָּבוֹא	Qal, imperfect *waw*-consecutive, third-person, feminine, singular (בּוֹא, to come, go)
אֵלֶיךָ	preposition, with pronominal suffix (second-person, masculine, singular)
תְּפִלָּתִי	noun, feminine, singular, construct (תְּפִלָּה, prayer), with pronominal suffix (first-person, common, singular)
אֶל	preposition
הֵיכַל	noun, masculine, singular, construct (הֵיכָל, palace, temple)

קׇדְשֶׁ֑ךָ   noun, masculine, singular, construct (קֹדֶשׁ, apartness, holiness), with pronominal suffix (second-person, masculine, singular)

Exegetical Notes:

1. Verse 8 contains another summary of Jonah's experience.

2. The preposition בְּ with the infinitive construct (הִתְעַטֵּף) is used to introduce an adverbial clause of time.

3. The verb עָטַף may describe physical fragility (Gen 30:42; Lam 2:11–12) but also spiritual disintegration (Ps 61:3; 77:4; Isa 57:16).

4. Note again the use of the preposition (עַל) with the pronominal suffix to maintain the stress pattern of the psalm.

5. Note that אֶת־יְהוָה, the direct object, is placed before the verb for emphasis. The object of Jonah's remembrance is more important than his remembering.

6. With respect to the verb זָכַר, Echols comments, "In the Old Testament, this verb often means not simply recollection, but taking a course of action. In this case, Jonah's remembrance is not simply to recall YHWH, but to pray to YHWH to deliver him from mortal danger."[19] The verb is often related to remembering God's covenant (e.g., Gen 9:15–16; Exod 2:24; Deut 5:15; 7:18; 8:18; Ps 25:6–7; 77:11; 103:18).

7. Note Echols' observation, "As in 2:3, the poet shifts from referring to YHWH in third-person speech (A) to second-person (B). The transition bespeaks a greater spiritual proximity of YHWH in Jonah's spirit, and perhaps alludes to the restoration of his pre-flight intimacy with YHWH."[20]

---

19. Echols, *Reading Jonah*, 46.
20. Echols, *Reading Jonah*, 47.

Jonah Prays

VERSE 9

Hebrew Text and Translation:

מְשַׁמְּרִים הַבְלֵי־שָׁוְא חַסְדָּם יַעֲזֹבוּ׃

Those who keep (revere) vain idols
are abandoning their (own) kindness.

Grammatical Analysis:

מְשַׁמְּרִים	Piel, participle active, masculine, plural, absolute (שָׁמַר, to keep)
הַבְלֵי	noun, masculine, plural, construct (הֶבֶל, vapour, breath)
שָׁוְא	noun, masculine, singular, absolute (שָׁוְא, vanity, emptiness)
חַסְדָּם	noun, masculine, singular, construct (חֶסֶד, mercy, kindness), with pronominal suffix (third-person, masculine, plural)
יַעֲזֹבוּ	Qal, imperfect, third-person, masculine, plural (עָזַב, to abandon, forsake)

Exegetical Notes:

1. Translators and commentators have struggled to understand this verse.[21] Despite the different translations in the versions, the Hebrew grammar of the passage is plain enough. However, since interpreters found it difficult to understand the meaning of the passage in its context they have come up with a variety of opinions.

---

21. For a fuller discussion of this verse, see Ferreira, "Note on Jonah 2.8."

2. We want to propose that Israel is being addressed. The intended audience of the book of Jonah was Israelite. The "keepers of vain idols" is a description or a critique of Israel. In other words, the verse does not just describe Jonah but Israel in general.

3. Note the expression "their kindness." The kindness under question is not Yahweh's kindness or a veiled reference to Yahweh; rather, the text refers to the kindness or mercy that should be present within the covenant community.

4. The term חֶסֶד occurs 246 times in the Old Testament and is a key theological word. It mostly refers to Yahweh's covenant mercy and loyalty towards his people Israel and has been variously translated as "loyalty," "faithfulness," "kindness," "grace," "mercy," and the traditional "loving-kindness." In Jonah 4:2 the term is used to describe an attribute of Yahweh. However, the term not only relates to a divine attribute, but it also functions on a human plane. It was expected that God's people show חֶסֶד to one another (Isa 57:1; Prov 3:3; 11:17; 19:22; 20:6).

5. In Hosea, Yahweh's charge against Israel is that there is no faithfulness, mercy, or knowledge of Yahweh in the land (Hos 4:1). Likewise, Amos reprimands the covenant community for its injustice and corruption (cf. Amos 2:6–8; 3:15; 4:1; 5:11; 5:15; 5:24; 6:1–4; 6:12; 8:4–6). In other words, in the eighth-century prophets, there is a persistent and strong accusation that Israel had abandoned the Lord and had no kindness. Instead, the nation had adopted idols and fostered corruption and injustice. It is in this canonical context that Jonah should be read.

6. How does the passage relate to the overall theme of the book? The main point of the author is that Jonah—Israel—does not understand the Lord's great concern to extend mercy to all people. Jonah was reluctant to carry out the Lord's mission because he knew that the Lord was "a gracious and compassionate God, slow to anger and abounding in love" (Jonah 4:2)—a graciousness which extends even to gentiles. The

Jonah Prays

idolatry of economic progress (materialism), nationalism, and dogmatic ideology caused Israel to abandon the weighty matters of the law—compassion, mercy, and justice.

7. It is interesting to note that the book of Jonah in the Leningrad Codex contains 688 words. The first word of the monocolon is word number 344. The final editor of the story may have inserted an editorial comment at the center of the story capturing the main problem that the book was addressing. The center of the narrative will be an apt location to state the main issue being addressed. By following idols, the people of Israel are abandoning basic humanity and kindness.

8. Another observation that may underscore careful construction on the part of the author or final editor is that the mono-colon here consists of twenty-two letters, the number of letters in the Hebrew alphabet.

VERSE 10

Hebrew Text and Translation:

וַאֲנִ֗י בְּק֤וֹל תּוֹדָה֙ אֶזְבְּחָה־לָּ֔ךְ אֲשֶׁ֥ר נָדַ֖רְתִּי אֲשַׁלֵּ֑מָה יְשׁוּעָ֖תָה לַיהוָֽה׃ ס

Therefore, I, with the voice of thanksgiving,
let me sacrifice to You;
what I have vowed let me fulfill.

Salvation *belongs* to the Lord!"

Grammatical Analysis:

וַאֲנִ֗י	first personal pronoun, singular, with the conjunction
בְּק֤וֹל	noun, masculine, singular, absolute (קוֹל, sound, voice), with preposition בְּ

The Book of Jonah

תּוֹדָה	noun, feminine, singular, absolute (תּוֹדָה, thanksgiving)
אֶזְבְּחָה	Qal, imperfect (cohortative), first-person, common, singular (זָבַח, to sacrifice)
לְךָ	preposition, with pronominal suffix (second-person, masculine singular)
אֲשֶׁר	relative pronoun
נָדַרְתִּי	Qal, perfect, first-person, common, singular (נָדַר, to vow)
אֲשַׁלֵּמָה	Piel, imperfect (cohortative), first-person, common, singular (שָׁלֵם, to complete, to requite)
יְשׁוּעָתָה	noun, feminine, singular, absolute (יְשׁוּעָה, salvation)
לַיהוָה	proper name, "Yahweh," or conventionally "the LORD," with preposition לְ

Exegetical Notes:

1. Verse 10 concludes the psalm. Lament has been transformed into thanksgiving and praise. It is clear that the psalm was composed after the fish released Jonah onto dry land (verse 11).

2. As the conclusion to the whole psalm, we may translate the conjunction *waw* as "therefore."

3. Note that the subject is placed before the verb. The author is emphasizing Jonah's personal experience and response to the Lord's salvation.

4. The prepositional phrase (בְּקוֹל תּוֹדָה) is also placed before the verb for emphasis. Sacrifice is not offered out of routine but from heartfelt thanksgiving.

5. It is interesting to observe that both verbs (אֶזְבְּחָה and אֲשַׁלֵּמָה) of the psalmist's prayer are in the cohortative. The psalmist prays that God will enable or allow him to offer praise and to fulfil his vows. Jonah, in light of his experience, recognizes

that all grace and strength stem from the Lord. Without the Lord's grace and strength, he would not be able to give thanks nor be able to fulfil his vows.

6. Thanksgiving is a subset of the peace offering (Lev 7:11–18). In the New Testament, we also experience God's peace through thanksgiving (cf. Phil 4:6–7).

7. The last line of the psalm, "Salvation belongs to the LORD!," is a noun sentence. It emphasizes an unchanging reality and spiritual truth. The salvation of God's people is totally dependent on the Lord's electing love, grace, and power. This creed occurs throughout the Bible (cf. Ps 3:8; 20:5; 21:1; 37:39; 38:22; 40:16; 68:19; 88:1; 95:1; 118:14; 119:41, 166). It encapsulates the biblical truth that salvation depends totally on the Lord's grace, initiative, action, and sustaining power. Of course, the term "salvation" (יְשׁוּעָתָה) is an echo of Jesus' name (יְהוֹשׁוּעַ).

8. A final observation on Jonah's prayer, which may be significant when we consider chapter 4, is that Jonah never actually acknowledges or confesses his sins. There are desperate cries for help and deliverance, and there is much confidence and hope, but there is no reminiscence of wrongdoing. Since God heard Jonah's prayer and delivered him, one may assume that there were some elements of confession in the prayer. However, elements of contrition and confession of wrong behavior are absent.

VERSE 11

Hebrew Text and Translation:

וַיֹּאמֶר יְהוָה לַדָּג
וַיָּקֵא אֶת־יוֹנָה אֶל־הַיַּבָּשָׁה׃ פ

Then the LORD spoke to the fish,
and it vomited Jonah out upon the dry land.

The Book of Jonah

Grammatical Analysis:

וַיֹּאמֶר	Qal, imperfect *waw*-consecutive, third-person, masculine, singular (אָמַר, to say)
יְהוָה	proper name, "Yahweh," or conventionally "the LORD"
לַדָּג	noun, masculine, singular, absolute (דָּג, fish), with the definite article and with the preposition לְ
וַיָּקֵא	Hifil, imperfect *waw*-consecutive, third-person, masculine, singular (קיא, to vomit up)
אֶת	direct object marker
יוֹנָה	proper name, "Jonah" (alternative meaning, "dove")
אֶל	preposition
הַיַּבָּשָׁה	noun, feminine, singular, absolute (יַבָּשָׁה, dry land), with the definite article

Exegetical Notes:

1. The resolution of Jonah's predicament occurs when the Lord speaks to the fish. We note that the Lord controls the situation and orchestrates deliverance for his prophet. There is grace even for a recalcitrant prophet.

2. The term קיא (to vomit) is a disgusting word (cf. Lev 18:28; Isa 19:14; 28:8; Jer 48:26; Job 20:15). Interestingly, the word is also used as a metaphor for Israel returning from the Babylonian exile (cf. Jer 51:31, 34, 44). The book of Jonah is not just about the deliverance of an individual prophet, it is about salvation history.

3. In the context of the story, we note that Jonah cried out to the Lord for salvation in the belly of the fish, but as we will soon observe, Jonah needed to learn more. Prayer and obedience are not enough, the Lord's prophet needed to come to a more intimate understanding of God.

Jonah Prays

4. In conclusion to our study of chapter 2, we may make a few observations on the significance of deliverance from the bowels of the fish. As mentioned before, the genre of the book of Jonah is historical narrative. Like the historical books in the Old Testament, the author or final editors of the text understood their narratives as relating historical events. They were not propagating myths or parables but historical realities. Denying the historical nature of these books rejects a critical aspect of Old Testament biblical theology. According to the biblical authors and our own experience, since the human predicament is intensely historical, incorporating both physical and spiritual aspects of human existence, so too salvation must be historical. The deliverance from Egypt, the promised land, and the Davidic kingdom were not just metaphors to live by but were experienced historical realities. A denial of this history is a rejection of the real essence of biblical theology. Within the canonical context the book of Jonah must not be separated from its salvation historical context. Since God is faithful, he breaks into history and nature in order to fulfil his covenantal promises for the salvation of his people. This is the significance of the "sign of Jonah" and the heart of the gospel (Matt 12:39–40): God loves the world so much that he is prepared to break into history and alter nature to achieve redemption for his elect. This is what happened two thousand years ago when the Word became flesh, died on the cross, and rose again on the third day. It is not just theology or a parable; it is historical and the start of a new creation. In other words, divine intervention—the miraculous—lies at the heart of the message of the book of Jonah, as it points forward to that greatest act in salvation history, the coming of the Lord Jesus Christ.

3

Jonah Preaches

VERSE 1

Hebrew Text and Translation:

וַיְהִי דְבַר־יְהוָה אֶל־יוֹנָה שֵׁנִית לֵאמֹר׃

Now the word of the LORD came to Jonah the second time, saying,

Grammatical Analysis:

וַיְהִי	Qal, imperfect *waw*-consecutive, third-person, masculine, singular (הָיָה, to be, become, is)
דְבַר	noun, masculine, singular, construct (דָּבָר, word, matter, thing)
יְהוָה	proper name, "Yahweh," or conventionally "the LORD"
אֶל	preposition, "to" or "towards"
יוֹנָה	proper name, "Jonah" (alternative meaning, "dove")
שֵׁנִית	adjective, feminine, singular, "a second *time*"

Jonah Preaches

לֵאמֹר   Qal, infinitive, construct, with suffix (אָמַר, to say), with preposition לְ

Exegetical Notes:

1. Chapter 3 verse 1 introduces the second section of the book of Jonah. God repeats his call. The Lord again initiates the action.
2. The first five words of the sentence are the same as in chapter 1 verse 1.
3. According to Wolff, in the context of chapter 2, "The way through death becomes a preparation for service."[1]
4. In the Bible, the notion of a "second time" speaks of grace (cf. Isa 11:11; Jer 13:3; 33:1; Hag 2:20).

VERSE 2

Hebrew Text and Translation:

קוּם לֵךְ אֶל־נִינְוֵה הָעִיר הַגְּדוֹלָה
וּקְרָא אֵלֶיהָ אֶת־הַקְּרִיאָה אֲשֶׁר אָנֹכִי דֹּבֵר אֵלֶיךָ:

"Arise, go to Nineveh, the great city,
and proclaim to it the proclamation which I am about to tell you."

Grammatical Analysis:

קוּם   Qal, imperative, second-person, masculine, singular (קוּם, to arise)

לֵךְ   Qal, imperative, second-person, masculine, singular (הָלַךְ, to go, walk)

---

1. Wolff, *Obadiah and Jonah*, 140.

The Book of Jonah

אֶל	preposition, "to" or "towards"
נִינְוֵה	proper noun, "Nineveh"
הָעִיר	noun, feminine, singular, absolute (עִיר, city), with definite article
הַגְּדוֹלָה	adjective, feminine, singular, absolute (גָּדוֹל, great), with definite article
וּקְרָא	Qal, imperative, second-person, masculine, singular (קָרָא, to cry, call, proclaim, read), with conjunction
אֵלֶיהָ	preposition, "to" or "towards," with pronominal suffix (third-person, feminine, singular)
אֶת	direct object marker
הַקְּרִיאָה	noun, feminine, singular, absolute (קְרִיאָה, proclamation)
אֲשֶׁר	relative pronoun
אָנֹכִי	first personal pronoun, singular, common
דֹּבֵר	Qal, participle, active, masculine, singular, absolute (דָּבַר, to speak)
אֵלֶיךָ	preposition, "to" or "towards," with pronominal suffix (second-person, masculine, singular)

Exegetical Notes:

1. Jonah is commanded a second time to go to Nineveh and make a proclamation against it. It is interesting to note that the content of the message is not specified.

2. Observe again that the first seven words are exactly the same as in chapter 1 verse 2, but the preposition עַל (upon) is substituted with אֶל (to). If one were to press a distinction between the two prepositions, עַל could be translated as "against it" and אֶל as "to it." In the first instance we may classify the

Jonah Preaches

preposition as expressing disadvantage and in the latter case as expressing advantage.²

3. The city name נִינְוֵה (Nineveh) occurs nine times in the book, seven of the occurrences are in chapter 3 (Jonah 1:1; 3:2, 3, 4, 5, 6, 7; 4:11).

4. The object marker אֵת (*nota accusativi*) introduces the direct object of the verb. The long vowel reduces to a short vowel (אֶת) because it becomes a linguistic unit with the following word (which is indicated by the *maqqeph*), thus losing its accent. The object marker is normally prefixed to nouns that are definite.³

5. Note the cognate accusative קְרִיאָה (proclamation) of the verb קָרָא (to proclaim).

6. The relative pronoun אֲשֶׁר defines the proclamation (קְרִיאָה). Note the subject is placed before the verb. A true prophet must speak God's message, so the subject enjoys the emphasis.⁴

7. The participle used as a verb may either indicate continuing action, action about to take place, or action in the future.⁵ According to the context here, we may translate it as "about to tell."

VERSE 3

Hebrew Text and Translation:

וַיָּקָם יוֹנָה וַיֵּלֶךְ אֶל־נִינְוֵה כִּדְבַר יְהוָה
וְנִינְוֵה הָיְתָה עִיר־גְּדוֹלָה לֵאלֹהִים מַהֲלַךְ שְׁלֹשֶׁת יָמִים׃

---

2. Cf. Echols, *Reading Jonah*, 55.

3. Nouns are definite when: 1) they have the article; 2) are part of a genitive construct chain; 3) have a pronominal suffix; 4) or are proper names.

4. Note the following passages on true vs false prophets: Deut 18:15–22; Jer 14:14; 23:9–40; Ezek 13:1–7; Matt 7:15–23.

5. Ferreira, *Old Testament Hebrew*, 40.

The Book of Jonah

So, Jonah arose and went to Nineveh, according to the word of the Lord. [Now Nineveh was an important city for God, a journey (mission) of three days.]

Grammatical Analysis:

וַיָּקָם	Qal, imperfect *waw*-consecutive, third-person, masculine, singular (קוּם, to arise)
יוֹנָה	proper name, "Jonah" (alternative meaning, "dove")
וַיֵּלֶךְ	Qal, imperfect *waw*-consecutive, third-person, masculine, singular (הָלַךְ, to walk, go)
אֶל	preposition, "to" or "towards"
נִינְוֵה	proper noun, "Nineveh"
כִּדְבַר	noun, masculine, singular, absolute (דָּבָר, word, matter, thing), with preposition כְּ
יְהוָה	proper name, "Yahweh," or conventionally "the LORD"
הָיְתָה	Qal, perfect, third-person, feminine, singular (הָיָה, to be, become, is)
עִיר	noun, feminine, singular, absolute (עִיר, city)
גְדוֹלָה	adjective, feminine, singular, absolute (גָּדוֹל, great)
לֵאלֹהִים	noun, masculine, plural, absolute (אֱלֹהִים, God), with preposition לְ
מַהֲלַךְ	noun, masculine, singular, construct (מַהֲלָךְ, walk, journey, going)
שְׁלֹשֶׁת	noun, feminine, singular, construct (שְׁלֹשָׁה, three)
יָמִים	noun, masculine, plural, absolute (יוֹם, day)

Exegetical Notes:

1. Unlike in chapter 1, this time Jonah obeys the word of the Lord and goes to Nineveh.

Jonah Preaches

2. The imperfect *waw*-consecutives (וַיָּקָם and וַיֵּלֶךְ) follow on as consequences of the Lord's command (קוּם לֵךְ).

3. The prepositional phrase כִּדְבַר יְהוָה ("according to the word of the LORD") is significant because it identifies Jonah as a true prophet. The most important qualification of being a true prophet is proclaiming the word of the LORD. The same phrase is also used in 2 Kgs 14:25 to describe the prophetic ministry of Jonah. Therefore, Jonah, despite his disobedience in chapter 1, is identified as a true prophet of the Lord.

4. The second line of verse 3 functions as a parenthesis. In translation one may place the sentence in brackets. Note that the subject נִינְוֵה (Nineveh) is placed before the verb and that the tense of the verb is perfect. We may translate the *waw* as "now." The sentence provides an additional description of the city, underscoring its significance for the author.

5. Note the direct or literal translation of the phrase, "a great city for God" (עִיר־גְּדוֹלָה לֵאלֹהִים). We understand the expression as more than just a superlative; the expression has more to do with theology than geography.[6] The translators of the Septuagint also understood the adjective in the same way (πόλις μεγάλη τῷ θεῷ).[7] The statement gives the reason Jonah was sent to Nineveh, which is theologically significant. Therefore, we translate the expression as "now Nineveh was an important city for God." The reason for Jonah's commission to go to Nineveh lies in the eternal divine decree rather than geopolitics.

6. Scholars are not sure how to understand or translate the final expression of the description, מַהֲלַךְ שְׁלֹשֶׁת יָמִים. The issue revolves around our understanding of the term (מַהֲלַךְ) "journey." Does it refer to the circumference or the diameter of the

---

6. Many translations render the expression simply as a superlative, "an exceedingly great city." However, there is no evidence for this use of the expression in Hebrew.

7. The Aramaic Targum Jonathan renders the expression as follows: "And Nineveh was a great city before the LORD" (וְנִינְוֵה הֲוַת קַרְתָּא רַבְּתָא קֳדָם יְיָ).

city, or perhaps to something else? In verse 4 it is stated that Jonah went into the city, a journey of one day (מַהֲלַךְ יוֹם אֶחָד). It is possible to understand the expression as a reference to the diameter or perhaps the length of the main road of the city, i.e., it will take a journey of three days to walk from one end to the other.[8] Generally, in the ancient world one day's journey on foot was roughly twenty-four to thirty kilometers.[9] The city would then have a main road eighty to ninety kilometers long![10] Another way to understand the reference to Nineveh is to interpret it as referring to all the surrounding cities of Nineveh. As such, Nineveh may refer to a whole region, not just to one walled city.[11] The term "city" could be a collective noun. Another possibility to consider, perhaps the best option, is that the term מַהֲלָךְ may refer to the time it will take to complete a specific mission (cf. Neh 2:6). In other words, Jonah's task would be a mission of three days. The expression then does not refer to the size of the city, but to the duration of Jonah's mission.[12] In this connection, Jonah's three-day mission provides a link with his experience of deliverance in chapter 2.

---

8. The term may refer to a walkway (Ezek 42:4).

9. According to Herodotus, a day's journey covers 150 stadia. Although ancient sources are not consistent and exact measurements differed, it appears that one stadium was roughly equivalent to 180 meters. Therefore, a day's journey covers around twenty-seven kilometers.

10. As mentioned previously, according to archaeological evidence, Sennacherib's Nineveh had a city wall of twelve kilometers in circumference. Nineveh appears to have been the largest city in the world at that time. It is also interesting to note that the cuneiform for the city name depicts a fish within a house. Many scholars believe that the name Nineveh possibly means "place of fish" or may relate to one of the fish deities associated with the Tigris River. For a comprehensive anthology of essays on ancient Nineveh, see Petit and Bonacossi, *Nineveh, the Great City*.

11. The expression "that is the great city" (הִוא הָעִיר הַגְּדֹלָה) in Gen 10:12 may refer to the whole region, including the cities of Nineveh, Rehoboth-ir, Calah, and Resen.

12. Chisholm, *Workbook for Intermediate Hebrew*, 70.

Jonah Preaches

VERSE 4

Hebrew Text and Translation:

וַיָּ֤חֶל יוֹנָה֙ לָב֣וֹא בָעִ֔יר מַהֲלַ֖ךְ י֣וֹם אֶחָ֑ד
וַיִּקְרָא֙ וַיֹּאמַ֔ר ע֚וֹד אַרְבָּעִ֣ים י֔וֹם וְנִֽינְוֵ֖ה נֶהְפָּֽכֶת׃

Then Jonah began to go through the city, one day's journey (mission). And he cried out and said,
"Yet forty days and Nineveh will be overthrown."

Grammatical Analysis:

וַיָּ֤חֶל	Hifil, imperfect *waw*-consecutive, third-person, masculine, singular (חָלַל, to pollute, to begin)
יוֹנָה	proper name, "Jonah" (alternative meaning, "dove")
לָבוֹא	Qal, infinitive, construct (בּוֹא, to come, to go), with preposition לְ
בָעִיר	noun, feminine, singular, absolute (עִיר, city), with definite article בְּ
מַהֲלַךְ	noun, masculine, singular, construct (מַהֲלַךְ, walk, journey, going)
יוֹם	noun, masculine, singular, absolute (יוֹם, day)
אֶחָד	adjective (numeral), masculine, singular, absolute (אֶחָד, one)
וַיִּקְרָא	Qal, imperfect *waw*-consecutive, third-person, masculine, singular (קָרָא, to proclaim)
וַיֹּאמַר	Qal, imperfect *waw*-consecutive, third-person, masculine, singular (אָמַר, to say)
עוֹד	adverb, "yet," "still," "again"
אַרְבָּעִים	noun (numeral), masculine, plural, absolute (אַרְבָּעִים, forty)

The Book of Jonah

יוֹם   noun, masculine, singular, absolute (יוֹם, day)

וְנִינְוֵה   proper noun, "Nineveh," with conjunction וְ

נֶהְפָּכֶת   Nifal, participle, active, feminine, singular, absolute (הָפַךְ, to turn, to overturn)

Exegetical Notes:

1. In verse 4 Jonah starts his mission with the message "yet forty days and Nineveh will be overthrown." We may assume that Jonah and the author are accurately relating the message that God communicated to Jonah. It is interesting to note that the message of five words follow the 3 + 2 stress pattern of Qinah lament, the pattern adopted in the psalm of chapter 2.

2. Considering what we mentioned above regarding the meaning of מַהֲלַךְ, the expression מַהֲלַךְ יוֹם אֶחָד may indicate the first day of Jonah's mission. The expression would then highlight the speed of the city's repentance.

3. It is interesting to note that instead of "yet forty days" the Septuagint reads, "yet three days" (Ἔτι τρεῖς ἡμέραι). For Snaith, this "makes much better sense."[13] The extant Hebrew manuscripts including the Dead Sea Scrolls as well as the Aramaic Targum Jonathan and the Greek Nahal Hever text all have "forty days." Nonetheless some of the church fathers were familiar with the "yet three days" reading of the Septuagint (e.g., Theodoret, Theodore, Jerome, Augustine).[14]

4. The Nifal participle here נֶהְפָּכֶת refers to future action.

5. It is important to point out that the verb הָפַךְ means "to turn" or "to overturn." In other words, it does not necessarily imply that Nineveh will be destroyed but just that it will be changed (i.e.,

---

13. Snaith, *Notes on the Hebrew Text of Jonah*, 32.

14. Some commentators have extended Jonah's "forty days" to a period of forty years between Jonah's proclamation in Nineveh and the destruction of Samaria in 722 BC, as well as the period between Jesus' crucifixion and the destruction of Jerusalem in AD 70.

Jonah Preaches

turned around or restored) after forty days (cf. 1 Kgs 22:34; Hos 7:8; Zeph 3:9). This is an example of double meaning.

6. The term הָפַךְ is also used in connection with the judgment and destruction of Sodom and Gomorrah (Deut 29:23).

7. In the flood story the expression "forty days" indicates a period of judgment upon the world (Gen 7:4,12). In Deut 9:18 it is used to refer to Moses' time of repentance on behalf of the Israelites.

8. One may speculate as to whether Jonah also proclaimed a message of repentance and forgiveness. One may assume that a message of judgment will imply the possibility of repentance and forgiveness to avert the impending judgment; otherwise, why would God send such a message? But, of course, God may send such a message of judgment to indicate that the subsequent judgment and destruction of the city came from him, so that his name may be glorified and to provide a warning to subsequent generations.

9. During the eighth century the people of Nineveh would have spoken Aramaic, which was a Semitic language and closely related to Hebrew. Jonah's coming from Northern Israel, close to the border of Aram (Syria), would probably have been able to converse in Aramaic. Official documents were written in Cuneiform script.

10. It is interesting to note the reference in the apocryphal book of Tobit, which was written in the third or second century BC, regarding Jonah's prophecy.[15] The elderly Tobit advised his children to flee Nineveh since the prophecy of Jonah regarding Nineveh's destruction was about to be fulfilled (Tobit 14:4, 8).

---

15. The book of Tobit in the apocrypha tells the story of Tobit, one of the exiles in Assyria.

The Book of Jonah

VERSE 5

Hebrew Text and Translation:

וַיַּאֲמִינוּ אַנְשֵׁי נִינְוֵה בֵּאלֹהִים וַיִּקְרְאוּ־צוֹם וַיִּלְבְּשׁוּ שַׂקִּים
מִגְּדוֹלָם וְעַד־קְטַנָּם:

Then the people of Nineveh believed in God, and they proclaimed a fast and put on sackcloth, from the greatest of them to the least of them.

Grammatical Analysis:

וַיַּאֲמִינוּ	Hifil, imperfect *waw*-consecutive, third-person, masculine, plural (אָמַן, to believe)
אַנְשֵׁי	noun, masculine, plural, construct (אִישׁ, man)
נִינְוֵה	proper noun, "Nineveh"
בֵּאלֹהִים	noun, masculine, plural, absolute (אֱלֹהִים, God), with preposition בְּ
וַיִּקְרְאוּ	Qal, imperfect *waw*-consecutive, third-person, masculine, plural (קָרָא, to proclaim)
צוֹם	noun, masculine, singular, absolute (צוֹם, fast)
וַיִּלְבְּשׁוּ	Qal, imperfect *waw*-consecutive, third-person, masculine, plural (לָבֵשׁ, to clothe)
שַׂקִּים	noun, masculine, plural, absolute (שַׂק, sackcloth)
מִגְּדוֹלָם	adjective, masculine, plural, construct (גָּדוֹל, great), with preposition מִן, with pronominal suffix (third-person, masculine, plural)
וְעַד	preposition (עַד, as far as, even to, up to), with conjunction וְ
קְטַנָּם	adjective, masculine, plural, construct (קָטָן, small), with pronominal suffix (third-person, masculine, plural)

Jonah Preaches

Exegetical Notes:

1. Verse 5 serves as a succinct summary statement, and then the following verses provide more detail. Whereas English composition usually provides a summary statement at the end, Hebrew narrative provides one at the beginning (cf. Gen 1:1; 39:2; Dan 1:9; 9:24).

2. Remarkably, the Ninevites responded positively and believed in God. It is not specified what exactly they believed. There could be at least three possibilities. They believed in the existence of Jonah's God, they believed that the city would be destroyed in forty days, or they believed that God might show compassion if they repented (or probably all three).

3. The verb אָמַן (to believe) merits further reflection. The basic idea of the root אמן conveys that which is firm or reliable.[16] In the Qal it means "to support" or "to nourish," and so as a substantive it often may denote a nurse (Num 11:12; Ruth 4:16; 2 Kgs 10:1) or refer to ones who are faithful (2 Sam 20:19; Ps 12:1; 31:23). In the Nifal it means "to establish" or "to be steadfast" (e.g., 2 Sam 7:16; Ps 78:8; 93:5). Most significant theologically is its use in the Hifil stem, where it conveys the meaning "to believe" or "to trust" (cf. Gen 15:6; Exod 4:8; Ps 27:13; 116:10; Isa 53:1).[17] It is important to note that whenever the verb is used to describe man's response to God, "it is based on God's signs (Exod 4:31), miracles (Ps 106:12), and word (Gen 15:6; Jonah 3:5)."[18] Believing in God assumes or implies a promise (אֱמֶת) on which the trust is based.[19] In

---

16. The cognates of the root אָמַת (faithfulness, truth; cf. Ps 117:2; Mic 7:20) and אֱמוּנָה (faith, faithfulness, trust; cf. Hab 2:4) are also theologically significant.

17. The perfect tense of the verb in the important passage in Gen 15:6 indicates that Abraham's faith was not just the result of the event in Gen 15—a once in a lifetime event—but a characteristic of his life since God called him in Gen 12:1-4.

18. See Jepsen, "אָמַן," 308.

19. According to Chisholm the Ninevites believed in the trustworthiness of God that he would destroy the city. But this would not explain the reason

The Book of Jonah

addition, when people are said to believe in God, their trust is always demonstrated in the context of the passage by appropriate action (e.g., Gen 15:6; Exod 4:31; Ps 106:12; Isa 28:16).[20] In the same way disbelief is demonstrated by disobedience (e.g., Num 14:11; Deut 9:23; Ps 78:32).

4. Moreover, the use of the Hifil, in distinction from the Qal or Nifal, probably means that the subject of the verb regards the object of the verb (i.e., the promise) as being trustworthy and reliable. Geerhardus Vos made the following interesting comment, "The Hiphil of *amen* here has a causative-productive sense, and the preposition brings out that the personal point at which this assurance sprang up was nothing else but the personal Jehovah, and that the same divine person, in whom it sprang up, was also the One in whom it came to rest."[21] To paraphrase Vos, Abraham's faith caused the promise to come into being or to be fulfilled, but the source of this power is the LORD Himself.[22] In the context of Abrahamic narrative, the promise relates to him having a son in whom the covenantal promises would be perpetuated. It appears that the definition in Hebrews 11:1 understands faith in an analogous way, "Now faith is the substance of things hoped for, the evidence of things not seen." Faith (i.e., trust in God's promises) is the substantiation of the promise of God, i.e., it is not just the verification of the promise, but it actually brings it about.

5. Observe the merismus, "from the greatest of them to the least of them." All the people of the city, those with high status as well as the ordinary people, came to believe in God.

6. Note Echols's comment on the use of גָּדוֹל: "The basic meaning of the adjective is 'great,' but used substantively as it is

---

for their repentance. See Chisholm, *Workbook for Intermediate Hebrew*, 73.

20. See Moberly "אָמַן," 1:432.

21. Vos, *Biblical Theology*, 84–85.

22. Abraham did not make himself believe. If this were the case one would have expected the Nifal or the Hithpael stem.

Jonah Preaches

here, it can convey the idea of courtiers or noblemen, as in 2 Kgs 10:6."[23]

7. With the verb יָרֵא the emphasis is on obedience; with the verb אָמַן the emphasis is on trust. The verb אָמַן is often used in connection with the events of salvation history (cf. Exod 14:31; Ps 106:12). As mentioned above, the use of the verb implies that the people of Nineveh acted on the promise or hope of deliverance, and their repentance, prayer, and change of behavior demonstrated appropriate action. In this regard, note that the Targum has "the people of Nineveh believed the Word of the LORD" (וְהֵימִינוּ אַנְשֵׁי נִינְוֵה בְּמֵימְרָא דַיָי). In other words, the translators of the Targum interpreted the Hebrew text to assume a promise of hope. Every translation is in some measure an interpretation.

8. Jonah's preaching is remarkably successful. The Ninevites responded much more positively to the message of the prophet than the people of Israel ever did.

VERSE 6

Hebrew Text and Translation:

וַיִּגַּע הַדָּבָר אֶל־מֶלֶךְ נִינְוֵה וַיָּקָם מִכִּסְאוֹ וַיַּעֲבֵר אַדַּרְתּוֹ מֵעָלָיו וַיְכַס שַׂק וַיֵּשֶׁב עַל־הָאֵפֶר׃

When the word reached the king of Nineveh, he arose from his throne, laid aside his robe from him, and covered himself with sackcloth and sat on the ashes.

Grammatical Analysis:

וַיִּגַּע   Qal, imperfect *waw*-consecutive, third-person, masculine, singular (נָגַע, to touch, reach, strike)

23. Echols, *Reading Jonah*, 64.

The Book of Jonah

הַדָּבָר	noun, masculine, singular, absolute (דָּבָר, word, matter, thing), with the definite article
אֶל	preposition, "to," "towards"
מֶלֶךְ	noun, masculine, singular, construct (מֶלֶךְ, king)
נִינְוֵה	proper noun, "Nineveh"
וַיָּקָם	Qal, imperfect *waw*-consecutive, third-person, masculine, singular (קוּם, to arise)
מִכִּסְאוֹ	noun, masculine, singular, construct (כִּסֵּא, chair, throne), with preposition מִן, with pronominal suffix (third-person, masculine, singular)
וַיַּעֲבֵר	Hifil, imperfect *waw*-consecutive, third-person, masculine, singular (עָבַר, to pass over)
אַדַּרְתּוֹ	noun, feminine, singular, construct (אַדֶּרֶת, mantle, cloak), with pronominal suffix (third-person, masculine, singular)
מֵעָלָיו	preposition (עַל, upon), with preposition מִן, and with pronominal suffix (third-person, masculine, singular)
וַיְכַס	Piel, imperfect *waw*-consecutive, third-person, masculine, singular (כָּסָה, to cover)
שַׂק	noun, masculine, singular, absolute (שַׂק, sack, sack-cloth)
וַיֵּשֶׁב	Qal, imperfect *waw*-consecutive, third-person, masculine, singular (יָשַׁב, to sit, remain, dwell)
עַל	preposition (עַל, upon)
הָאֵפֶר	noun, masculine, plural, absolute (אֵפֶר, ashes), with the definite article

Jonah Preaches

Exegetical Notes:

1. As mentioned above, we regard verse 5 as a summary statement, so verse 6 may be regarded as a flashback or a more detailed description of how the events transpired.

2. It is interesting to note the use of the verb נָגַע (touch, reach, strike). The message (הַדָּבָר) of the prophet not only reached the king but touched or moved his heart (cf. 1 Sam 10:26; Ps 73:14; Isa 53:4). The king was emotionally and spiritually affected by the message. We note here the power of God's word to effect change.

3. It is also interesting to observe the use of the verb קוּם "to arise" in the book of Jonah. The verb occurs six times in the book (Jonah 1:2, 3, 6; 3:2, 3, 6). The human action of "rising" is always in response to God's word. God's initiative causes a reaction among human beings. The term is also significant in terms of salvation history (cf. Gen 17:7, 19; Exod 12:31; Num 24:17; Deut 2:13, 24; 18:15, 18; 34:10; Dan 2:39, 44). In the New Testament, the redemptive significance of the term reaches its climax with the resurrection of Jesus from the dead.

4. The king rose from his throne and sat in the dust as a gesture of humility.

5. Note the use of the Hifil with the verb וַיַּעֲבֵר (from עָבַר, to pass over). Kings were dressed by their attendants; after the king rose from his throne, he did not allow the royal garment to be put on him but had it passed over him as it were. Instead, the king put on sackcloth. The Piel (וַיְכַס) suggests that the king dressed himself with sackcloth.[24]

6. The reaction of the king of Nineveh is in sharp contrast to Jehoiakim, who was unmoved by Jeremiah's words (Jer 36:9–31).

---

24. The NKJV, NASB, and ESV also understand the text in the same way.

7. Scholars have pondered who this Assyrian king might have been. A possible suggestion is Ashur-dan III, who reigned from 773 to 756 BC. Although to date no Assyrian record of this event has thus far come to light, we do not doubt its historicity. Some commentators have speculated that it is unlikely for a king to behave in this way. But, of course, this is the point of the story: the reaction of the gentiles is both unexpected and remarkable.

VERSE 7

Hebrew Text and Translation:

וַיַּזְעֵק וַיֹּאמֶר בְּנִינְוֵה מִטַּעַם הַמֶּלֶךְ וּגְדֹלָיו לֵאמֹר הָאָדָם וְהַבְּהֵמָה הַבָּקָר וְהַצֹּאן אַל־יִטְעֲמוּ מְאוּמָה אַל־יִרְעוּ וּמַיִם אַל־יִשְׁתּוּ:

> Afterwards, he made a declaration and it said, "In Nineveh by the decree of the king and his nobles (saying): Do not let man, beast, i.e., herds or flocks, taste a thing. Do not let them eat or drink water."

Grammatical Analysis:

וַיַּזְעֵק	Hifil, imperfect *waw*-consecutive, third-person, masculine, singular (זָעַק, to call out, make a proclamation)
וַיֹּאמֶר	Qal, imperfect *waw*-consecutive, third-person, masculine, singular (אָמַר, to say)
בְּנִינְוֵה	proper noun, "Nineveh," with preposition בְּ
מִטַּעַם	noun, masculine, singular, construct (טַעַם, declaration, judgment, decree), with preposition מִן
הַמֶּלֶךְ	noun, masculine, singular, absolute (מֶלֶךְ, king), with the article

Jonah Preaches

וּגְדֹלָיו	adjective, masculine, plural, construct (גָּדוֹל, great), with conjunction וְ, with pronominal suffix (third-person, masculine, singular)
לֵאמֹר	Qal, infinitive, construct (אָמַר, to say), with preposition לְ
הָאָדָם	noun, masculine, singular, absolute (אָדָם, man, mankind), with the article
וְהַבְּהֵמָה	noun, feminine, singular, absolute (בְּהֵמָה, animal, cattle, livestock), with the conjunction, and with the article
הַבָּקָר	noun, masculine, singular, absolute (בָּקָר, cattle, herd, ox), with the article
וְהַצֹּאן	noun, masculine, singular, absolute (צֹאן, sheep), with the conjunction, and with the article
אַל	adverb, "not"
יִטְעֲמוּ	Qal, imperfect (jussive), third-person, masculine, plural (טָעַם, to taste)
מְאוּמָה	noun, feminine, absolute (מְאוּמָה, anything)
אַל	adverb, "not"
יִרְעוּ	Qal, imperfect (jussive), third-person, masculine, plural (רָעָה, to pasture, tend)
וּמַיִם	noun, masculine, plural, absolute (מַיִם, water), with the conjunction
אַל	adverb, "not"
יִשְׁתּוּ	Qal, imperfect (jussive), third-person, masculine, plural (שָׁתָה, to drink)

Exegetical Notes:

1. Verses 7 to 9 record the decree of the king in great detail.
2. The prepositional phrase "in Nineveh" (בְּנִינְוֵה) may either be part of the wording of the decree itself or be taken with the

verb (וַיֹּאמֶר) introducing the decree. The disjunctive accent *zaqeph qaton* (֔) above the phrase בְּנִינְוֵה in the Leningrad Codex text indicates that the Masoretic scribes preferred the latter option.[25] It seems more likely that the prepositional phrase is part of the decree since the context is clearly within the city of Nineveh. The injunction to repent applies only to Nineveh and not to the whole Assyrian empire.

3. In Persian times animals were included in mourning ceremonies (Herodotus 1.24; Plutarch, *Alexander* 72; Judith 4:10); this practice is unknown among the Assyrians, even though many royal letters of penitence have been discovered from ancient Assyria.

4. Observe the use of the Hifil וַיַּזְעֵק. The king caused a proclamation to be made. We may translate the copula *waw* as "consequently," "afterwards" or "therefore." The subject of the verb וַיֹּאמֶר according to the context is the decree.

5. Note that the decree placed a prohibition on people and livestock (הָאָדָם וְהַבְּהֵמָה). The term אָדָם refers to people and is used here as a collective noun.[26] The term בְּהֵמָה here is a collective noun and refers to domesticated animals or livestock.[27] The words הַבָּקָר וְהַצֹּאן stand in apposition to "livestock" (הַבְּהֵמָה) and provide a more detailed explanation of what livestock are included.

VERSE 8

Hebrew Text and Translation:

וְיִתְכַּסּוּ שַׂקִּים הָאָדָם וְהַבְּהֵמָה וְיִקְרְאוּ אֶל־אֱלֹהִים בְּחָזְקָה וְיָשֻׁבוּ אִישׁ מִדַּרְכּוֹ הָרָעָה וּמִן־הֶחָמָס אֲשֶׁר בְּכַפֵּיהֶם:

---

25. The disjunctive accents indicate divisions in the text; it is like a separator mark between two segments of a line.

26. The LXX has Οἱ ἄνθρωποι (plural: the people).

27. The LXX has τὰ κτήνη (plural: the animals).

Jonah Preaches

"But let both man and beast cover themselves with sack-cloth; and let them call on God earnestly,
and let each turn from his wicked way and from the violence which is in their hands."

Grammatical Analysis:

וְיִתְכַּסּוּ	Hithpael, imperfect, third-person, masculine, plural (כָּסָה, to cover)
שַׂקִּים	noun, masculine, plural, absolute (שַׂק, sack, sack-cloth)
הָאָדָם	noun, masculine, singular, absolute (אָדָם, man, humanity), with the article
וְהַבְּהֵמָה	noun, feminine, singular, absolute (בְּהֵמָה, animal, cattle, livestock), with the article, and with the conjunction
וְיִקְרְאוּ	Qal, imperfect (jussive), third-person, masculine, plural (קָרָא, to cry, call, proclaim, read)
אֶל	preposition
אֱלֹהִים	noun, masculine, plural, absolute (אֵל, God)
בְּחָזְקָה	noun, feminine, singular, absolute (חָזְקָה, strength, force), with preposition בְּ
וְיָשֻׁבוּ	Qal, imperfect (jussive), third-person, masculine, plural (שׁוּב, to turn, repent)
אִישׁ	noun, masculine, singular, absolute (אִישׁ, man, each)
מִדַּרְכּוֹ	noun, masculine, singular, construct (דֶּרֶךְ, way), with the preposition מִן, and with the pronominal suffix (third-person, masculine, singular)
הָרָעָה	noun, feminine, singular, absolute (רַע, bad, evil), with the definite article
וּמִן	preposition, with the conjunction
הֶחָמָס	noun, masculine, singular, absolute (חָמָס, violence), with the definite article

The Book of Jonah

אֲשֶׁר   relative pronoun

בְּכַפֵּיהֶם   noun, masculine, dual, construct (כַּף, palm, hand), with the preposition בְּ, and with the pronominal suffix (third-person, masculine, plural)

Exegetical Notes:

1. We translated the *waw* as an adversative conjunction: people and livestock should not eat or drink anything, but instead cry out to God. Also note the use of the Hithpael jussive יִתְכַּסּוּ. The use of the Hithpael implies a reciprocal meaning, i.e., "let them cover one another." In this way the animals will be covered with sackcloth by the people.

2. Note that the phrase הַבָּקָר וְהַצֹּאן in verse 7 is omitted here since בְּהֵמָה has already been explained in the previous verse.

3. The prepositional phrase בְּחָזְקָה is used adverbially (lit: "with strength"). Biblical Hebrew does not employ many adverbs (apart from the common adverbials, כֹּה, הִנֵּה, אַךְ, אָז, אַל, לֹא, שָׁם, פֹּה, etc.).

4. Similar to the description of the repentance of the sailors in chapter 1, the description of the repentance of the inhabitants of Nineveh is genuine and thorough. The Ninevites' external ceremonial penitence (יִתְכַּסּוּ שַׂקִּים) is attendant with much earnest prayer (יִקְרְאוּ אֶל־אֱלֹהִים בְּחָזְקָה) as well as a change in behavior (יָשֻׁבוּ אִישׁ מִדַּרְכּוֹ הָרָעָה).

5. Note that the inhabitants of Nineveh needed to repent from their evil individually (note singular suffix, מִדַּרְכּוֹ) as well as their collective propensity towards violence (note plural suffix, בְּכַפֵּיהֶם). As mentioned, the Assyrians had a reputation for cruelty and violence.

Jonah Preaches

VERSE 9

Hebrew Text and Translation:

מִי־יוֹדֵעַ יָשׁוּב וְנִחַם הָאֱלֹהִים וְשָׁב מֵחֲרוֹן אַפּוֹ וְלֹא נֹאבֵד:

"Who knows, God may turn and relent (have mercy), and after that turn away from His burning anger so that we may not perish?"

Or

The God who knows will turn and relent, and so turn aside from His fierce anger and we will not perish."

Grammatical Analysis:

מִי	interrogative adverb, "who"
יוֹדֵעַ	Qal, participle, active, masculine, singular (יָדַע, to know)
יָשׁוּב	Qal, imperfect, third-person, masculine, singular (שׁוּב, to turn, repent)
וְנִחַם	Nifal, perfect *waw*-consecutive, third-person, masculine, singular (נחם, to relent, be sorry)
הָאֱלֹהִים	noun, masculine, plural, absolute (אֵל, God), with the definite article
וְשָׁב	Qal, perfect *waw*-consecutive, third-person, masculine, singular (שׁוּב, to turn, repent)
מֵחֲרוֹן	noun, masculine, singular, construct (חָרוֹן, anger), with the preposition מִן
אַפּוֹ	noun, masculine, singular, absolute (אַף, nostril, nose, anger), with the pronominal suffix (third-person, masculine, singular)
וְלֹא	adverb "not," with the conjunction

נֹאבֵד Qal, imperfect, first-person, common, plural (אָבַד, to perish)

Exegetical Notes:

1. It seems that verse 9 expresses the wish of the king and the nobles of Nineveh. But the statement may also be regarded as a question expressing doubt or as an assertion about God's knowledge and plan. The interpreter must make an exegetical decision. A question expressing doubt seems to fit the context better.

2. The theological question posed by the king and the nobles ("who knows") indicates that they are not sure of the outcome of their repentance.

3. Note that הָאֱלֹהִים is used with the article.

4. The verb נָחַם has raised many theological questions in the history of interpretation. In the Nifal stem it may mean "to be sorry," "to have compassion," "to console oneself" or "to be comforted." The root occurs 119 times in the Old Testament.

5. The LXX has "who knows if God will reconsider (μετανοέω, repent) and turn away from His anger . . . ?"

6. The second line indicates the hopeful result of God's reconsideration.

7. The first four words of the verse also occur in Joel 2:14, where it is used as an encouragement for Israel to repent.

8. We will provide a more in-depth consideration of the verb נחם (to relent, be sorry) in the next verse.

Jonah Preaches

VERSE 10

Hebrew Text and Translation:

וַיַּרְא הָאֱלֹהִים אֶת־מַעֲשֵׂיהֶם כִּי־שָׁבוּ מִדַּרְכָּם הָרָעָה וַיִּנָּחֶם הָאֱלֹהִים עַל־הָרָעָה אֲשֶׁר־דִּבֶּר לַעֲשׂוֹת־לָהֶם וְלֹא עָשָׂה:

When God saw their deeds, that they turned from their wicked way, then God relented (had mercy) concerning the calamity which He had declared to do to them, and He did not do *it*.

Grammatical Analysis:

וַיַּרְא	Qal, imperfect *waw*-consecutive, third-person, masculine, singular (רָאָה, to see, observe)
הָאֱלֹהִים	noun, masculine, plural, absolute (אֵל, God), with the definite article
אֶת	direct object marker
מַעֲשֵׂיהֶם	noun, masculine, plural, construct (מַעֲשֶׂה, deed, work, labour)
כִּי	conjunction, introducing the object of verbs of perception "that"
שָׁבוּ	Qal, perfect, third-person, common, plural (שׁוּב, to turn, repent)
מִדַּרְכָּם	noun, masculine, singular, construct (דֶּרֶךְ, way), with the preposition מִן, and with the pronominal suffix (third-person, masculine, plural)
הָרָעָה	noun, feminine, singular, absolute (רַע, bad, evil), with the definite article
וַיִּנָּחֶם	Nifal, imperfect *waw*-consecutive, third-person, masculine, singular (נחם, to relent, be sorry)

The Book of Jonah

הָאֱלֹהִים	noun, masculine, plural, absolute (אֵל, God), with the definite article
עַל	preposition, "upon"
הָרָעָה	noun, feminine, singular, absolute (רַע, bad, evil), with the definite article
אֲשֶׁר	relative pronoun
דִּבֶּר	Piel, perfect, third-person, masculine, singular (דִּבֶּר, to speak)
לַעֲשׂוֹת	Qal, infinitive, construct (עָשָׂה, to do, make), with preposition לְ
לָהֶם	preposition לְ, with the pronominal suffix (third-person, masculine, plural)
וְלֹא	adverb "not," with the conjunction
עָשָׂה	Qal, perfect, third-person, masculine, singular (עָשָׂה, to do, make)

Exegetical Notes:

1. In verse 10, God indeed relents from judging the city and its people. Verse 10 is a complex sentence: the first part with the imperfect *waw*-consecutive introduces a circumstantial clause, and the second part contains the main clause. The main clause in turn may be regarded as a compound sentence consisting of a complex and a simple sentence.

2. Note that the conjunction כִּי here introduces the object clause of verbs of saying, seeing, and hearing, "that." God saw that the people of Nineveh repented.

3. Note the use of the perfect שָׁבוּ in the object clause, "they had turned" (pluperfect). In other words, some time had elapsed between their repenting and God's seeing. Any genuine turning away from sin must be a lasting turning away from sin.

Jonah Preaches

Like the repentance of the sailors in chapter 1, the author portrays the repentance of the Ninevites as a true repentance.

4. Students should also note the use of perfect tenses in the last two clauses (אֲשֶׁר־דִּבֶּר לַעֲשׂוֹת־לָהֶם וְלֹא עָשָׂה). God relented concerning the calamity which he had spoken (דִּבֶּר, pluperfect) previously. And the result was that "He did not do it" (עָשָׂה, past tense). The action, or non-action, of the verb עָשָׂה occurred after the action of God's proclamation indicated by the verb דִּבֶּר.

5. Some translations render the expression וַיִּנָּחֶם הָאֱלֹהִים as God "changing his mind" (NLT, GNT, NRSV). However, we must refute such an interpretation. From a theological point of view, this verse must be interpreted in light of the rest of Scripture, which teaches that God is sovereign, all-knowing, and immutable (Num 23:19; 1 Sam 15:29; Ps 33:11; 102:27; Isa 46:10; Mal 3:6; Eph 1:11; 2 Tim 2:13; Heb 6:17; 13:8; Jas 1:17). Strictly speaking, God does not change his mind.

6. The verb נחם is used with a number of nuances in the Old Testament (e.g., to be remorseful, to regret, to turn, to be sorry, to feel sorrow or be compassionate); it never refers to God changing his mind or to God repenting.[28] Perhaps, in verse 9 the men of Nineveh may have applied the idea of repentance or change (שׁוּב) to God, but surely their understanding of God is problematic. In verse 10 the inspired author describes God's reaction to the Ninevites' repentance (שׁוּב): instead of judging the city, God showed mercy. The verb שׁוּב (to change or to repent) is not applied to God's action in verse 10.[29] The final clause or sentence in verse 10 (וְלֹא עָשָׂה) further explains God's action, i.e., he did not do what he threatened he would do.

---

28. Echols writes, "Clearly God is never in need of repentance in the usual understanding of the word. Rather, the idea here is more of relenting." See Echols, *Reading Jonah*, 67.

29. The Septuagint very inappropriately has God repenting (καὶ μετενόησεν ὁ θεὸς ἐπὶ τῇ κακίᾳ).

7. We may quote John Calvin's comments on this verse by way of explanation:

> Now as to what Jonah adds, that God was led to repent, it is a mode of speaking that ought to be sufficiently known to us. Strictly speaking, no repentance can belong to God: and it ought not to be ascribed to his secret and hidden counsel. God then is in himself ever the same, and consistent with himself; but he is said to repent, when a regard is had to the comprehension of men: for as we conceive God to be angry, whenever he summons us to his tribunal, and shows to us our sins; so also, we conceive him to be placable, when he offers the hope of pardon. But it is according to our perceptions that there is any change, when God forgets his wrath, as though he had put on a new character. As then we cannot otherwise be terrified, that we may be humbled before God and repent, except he sets forth before us his wrath, the Scripture accommodates itself to the grossness of our understanding. But, on the other hand, we cannot confidently call on God, unless we feel assured that he is placable. We hence see that some kind of change appears to us, whenever God either threatens or gives hope of pardon and reconciliation: and to this must be referred this mode of speaking which Jonah adopts, when he says that God repented.[30]

8. In other words, passages in the Bible which speak of God's "regret" describe how God's actions appear to man (cf. Gen 6:6; Exod 32:14; 1 Sam 15:11; 2 Sam 24:16; Ps 106:45). However, strictly speaking, God does everything appropriate to the situation, whether bestowing blessing or punishment, which is in accordance with his sovereign will.[31] As explained above by Calvin, Scripture speaks in this way to reveal to us that God is personal and to encourage the faithful to respond to God with repentance and faith.

---

30. Calvin, *John Calvin Bible Commentaries*, 86.

31. Or one may say that God changed his mind in accordance with his nature and sovereign will, cf. Jer 18:7–10.

9. Therefore, "relent" is probably the best translation for the term נחם here in English, but by relenting we mean that God showed mercy (undeserved favour) rather than compassion (which implies some measure of merit or attractiveness in those receiving compassion).[32] Since the idea of a change in mind cannot and should not be applied to God, it is therefore better to understand the verb as showing mercy.

10. Finally, the comment in the *Reformation Study Bible* is also helpful: "When the Bible narrates God's actions, it often does so in anthropomorphic terms, i.e., ascribing to God human characteristics. This change in God's actions does not imply a change in his sovereign will. The Lord's apparent change of mind (i.e., his sovereign choice to carry out his own action in a way that is appropriate to a human response) is fully compatible with God's sovereignty and immutability, since he ordains the means as well as the ends of his sovereign will (Jer 18:7–10)."[33]

---

32. The best translations have preferred this rendering (cf. NIV, ESV, NKJV, NASB, Amplified Bible, CSB, NET Bible).

33. Sproul, *Reformation Study Bible*, 1568.

4

Jonah Complains

VERSE 1

Hebrew Text and Translation:

וַיֵּרַע אֶל־יוֹנָה רָעָה גְדוֹלָה וַיִּחַר לוֹ׃

But it greatly displeased Jonah and he became angry.
Lit. And it was a great annoyance (displeasure) for Jonah, and so it angered him (or, "and so he became angry because of it").

Grammatical Analysis:

וַיֵּרַע	Qal, imperfect *waw*-consecutive, third-person, masculine, singular (רָעַע, to be displeasing, to be bad)
אֶל	preposition
יוֹנָה	proper name, "Jonah" (alternative meaning, "dove")
רָעָה	noun, feminine, singular, absolute (רָעָה, evil, misery, distress)
גְדוֹלָה	adjective, feminine, singular, absolute (גָּדוֹל, great)

Jonah Complains

וַיִּחַר   Qal, imperfect *waw*-consecutive, third-person, masculine, singular (חָרָה, to burn, be angry)

לוֹ   preposition, with the pronominal suffix (third-person, singular, masculine)

Exegetical Notes:

1. In the following verses the author records Jonah's reaction to God sparing Nineveh. Chisholm notes, "Apparently God revealed to Jonah his decision to relent from sending judgment upon Nineveh."[1] Or, since the city was not destroyed after the designated period it become obvious to Jonah that God relented.

2. In the first section of the book, the author emphasizes Jonah's action in response to the Lord's commission. In the second section of the book, the author emphasizes Jonah's emotional reaction to God sparing Nineveh. Again, Jonah's response comes as a surprise to the reader. In general, true prophets surely obey the call of the Lord and are pleased when people repent of their evil ways. Why is the prophet's response in chapter 1 and in chapter 4 so unusual? Various answers have been offered, but most are unconvincing. For example, 1) Jonah was terrified to go on an arduous journey and face the notorious Assyrians, but boarding a ship to go to Tarshish appears to be more perilous, and under the threat of death Jonah remained calm. 2) Jonah scrupulously kept the kosher laws and did not want to defile himself interacting with gentiles, but Jonah has no problem boarding a gentile ship and never showed any animosity towards the sailors on the ship. 3) Jonah hated the gentiles and did not want them to be saved, but Jonah was prepared to give his life for the gentile sailors on the ship (some have even accused Jonah of theological racism or theological parochialism!). 4) Jonah was concerned

---

1. Chisholm, *Workbook for Intermediate Hebrew*, 81.

that his reputation would be tarnished if the prophecy of destruction would not be fulfilled, but Jonah acknowledged his disobedience openly to the gentiles on the ship; he confessed his shortcomings. 5) Jonah wished that God would destroy the Ninevites because they would later destroy the kingdom of Israel, but the book of Jonah never casts Nineveh in this light (the Assyrians destroyed Samaria in 722 BC). 6) Another suggestion is that Jonah feared that when Israel heard that God spared Nineveh, they themselves (i.e., the Israelites) would not repent of their sins and would presume on God's compassion, however, chapter 3 clearly states that God relented because the Ninevites repented of their evil ways so the Israelites would not have come to that conclusion.

3. Note that Jonah is the indirect object in the first part of the sentence. The subject of the verb is implied by the context, "it," i.e., God relenting from judging the city of Nineveh.

4. The verb רָעַע means "to be bad," "to be evil," or "to be displeasing." In the context here it means to be displeasing (cf. Num 11:10; 22:34; Josh 24:15). It is a denominative verb, i.e., the verb is derived from the noun רָעָה.

5. It is interesting to note the author's play on words. Jonah is sent to Nineveh on account of its evil (Jonah 1:2; רָעָה). But now, after God relents from punishing the Ninevites, it becomes an evil thing for Jonah. Chisholm comments, "Ironically, at the beginning of the story the word characterized the evil of the Ninevites; by the end of the story, it applies to Jonah."[2]

6. The noun רָעָה has different nuances according to the context (e.g., trouble, calamity, evil, misery, distress, injury). The translator or interpreter must make a decision in each case.[3]

---

2. Chisholm, *Workbook for Intermediate Hebrew*, 87. Also note the frequent use of רָעָה and the adjective רַע with different nuances in the book of Jonah (1:2, 7, 8; 3:8, 10; 4:1, 2, 6). As a general rule one must translate the same Hebrew word consistently throughout a narrative. However, context is always primary and sometimes demands that we use a different English word.

3. Of course, students should avoid the exegetical error of "totality transfer," which means to apply every possible meaning of the word to every use of the

Jonah Complains

7. The verb חָרָה means "to be angry." Some scholars also regard it as a denominative verb.

8. There are two possible ways to interpret the last clause. The subject may still be "it," i.e., God relenting from judging the city of Nineveh, and then the preposition with the pronominal suffix (לוֹ) indicates the indirect object of the verb which refers again to "him," i.e., to Jonah. In this way the syntactical structure of the second clause reflects that of the first. Another possibility would be to regard Jonah as the subject of the verb, and then the preposition with the pronominal suffix (לוֹ) indicates the direct object of the verb and refers to "it," i.e., God relenting from judging the city of Nineveh (NASB, ESV, NKJV, YLT, GB). The preposition לְ is sometimes used instead of the direct object marker to introduce the object of the verb. In the Septuagint, Jonah is the subject of both verbs.[4]

VERSE 2

Hebrew Text and Translation:

וַיִּתְפַּלֵּל אֶל־יְהוָֹה וַיֹּאמַר
אָנָּה יְהוָה הֲלוֹא־זֶה דְבָרִי עַד־הֱיוֹתִי עַל־אַדְמָתִי
עַל־כֵּן קִדַּמְתִּי לִבְרֹחַ תַּרְשִׁישָׁה כִּי יָדַעְתִּי
כִּי אַתָּה אֵל־חַנּוּן וְרַחוּם אֶרֶךְ אַפַּיִם וְרַב־חֶסֶד וְנִחָם עַל־הָרָעָה׃

> Then he prayed to the LORD and said,
> "Please LORD, was this not my complaint while I was still in my own land? Therefore, I went out early at first to flee towards Tarshish, for I knew that You are a God of grace and compassion, slow to anger and abundant in lovingkindness, and one who frequently relents concerning calamity.

---

word in a text. This error is not to be confused with the literary device of double meaning (double entendre), which is a deliberate play on words by the author.

4. The LXX reads: Καὶ ἐλυπήθη Ιωνας λύπην μεγάλην καὶ συνεχύθη ("And Jonah became angry with great anger, and he became confused").

The Book of Jonah

Grammatical Analysis:

וַיִּתְפַּלֵּל	Hithpael, imperfect *waw*-consecutive, third-person masculine, singular (פָּלַל, to intervene, pray)
אֶל	preposition
יְהוָה	proper name, "Yahweh," or conventionally "the LORD"
וַיֹּאמַר	Qal, imperfect *waw*-consecutive, third-person, masculine, singular (אָמַר, to say)
אָנָּה	particle of entreaty
יְהוָה	proper name, "Yahweh," or conventionally "the LORD"
הֲלוֹא	adverb "not," with interrogative הֲ
זֶה	demonstrative pronoun (masculine, singular)
דְבָרִי	noun, masculine, singular, construct (דָּבָר, word, matter, thing), with the pronominal suffix (first-person, common, singular)
עַד	preposition
הֱיוֹתִי	Qal, infinitive, construct (הָיָה, to be, become, is), with the pronominal suffix (first-person, common, singular)
עַל	preposition
אַדְמָתִי	noun, masculine, singular, absolute (אֲדָמָה, ground, earth, country), with the pronominal suffix (first-person, common, singular)
עַל	preposition
כֵּן	adverb, "thus" or "so"
קִדַּמְתִּי	Piel, perfect, first-person, common, singular (קָדַם, to be in front, rise early, do for the first time, meet, anticipate, forestall)
לִבְרֹחַ	Qal, infinitive, construct (בָּרַח, to flee), with the preposition לְ
תַּרְשִׁישָׁה	proper noun "Tarshish," with directional ה
כִּי	conjunction, "because"

Jonah Complains

יָדַעְתִּי	Qal, perfect, first-person, common, singular (יָדַע, to know)
כִּי	conjunction, "that"
אַתָּה	second personal pronoun, singular
אֵל	noun, masculine, plural, absolute (אֵל, God)
חַנּוּן	adjective, masculine, singular, absolute (חַנּוּן, gracious)
וְרַחוּם	adjective, masculine, singular, absolute (רַחוּם, compassionate), with conjunction
אֶרֶךְ	adjective, masculine, singular, construct (אֶרֶךְ, long)
אַפַּיִם	noun, masculine, dual, absolute (אַף, nostril, nose)
וְרַב	adjective, masculine, singular, construct (רַב, much, great), with conjunction
חֶסֶד	noun, masculine, singular, absolute (חֶסֶד, goodness, kindness)
וְנִחָם	Nifal, participle, active, masculine, singular, absolute (נחם, to relent, be sorry)
עַל	preposition
הָרָעָה	noun, feminine, singular, absolute (רָעָה, distress, misery, evil), with the definite article

Exegetical Notes:

1. Jonah now prays to the Lord and complains about the Lord's goodness and grace.

2. Jonah's prayer begins with the address אָנָּה יְהוָה ("Please LORD!"). Note the particle of entreaty, אָנָּה (oh! please! now! I pray!). The particle of entreaty also occurs in the prayer of the sailors (Jonah 1:14). It is often followed by a request. Jonah's request follows in verse 3 (i.e., "please take my life"). The divine name is also in the vocative here. The first two words of Jonah's prayer are the same as the words of the gentiles in Jonah 1:14.

3. The sentence starts with the interrogative הֲ, making the whole statement a question.

4. The expression עַל־כֵּן means "therefore." Then, the causal clause, introduced with the conjunction כִּי, gives the reason for Jonah's complaint (דְבָרִי).

5. Note the use of the infinitive construct with the preposition to indicate a temporal clause, עַד־הֱיוֹתִי עַל־אַדְמָתִי ("while I was still in my own land").

6. Echols suggests that we may translate דְבָרִי as "my concern."[5] The NET Bible translated the word as "what I thought" taking it to refer to Jonah's inner speech.

7. Dictionaries provide a range of meanings for the verb קָדַם, including "to be in front," "to meet," "to approach," "to do early," "to do for the first time," and "to forestall."[6] It is a denominative verb from קֶדֶם, meaning "east." The Septuagint translated the verb with προφθάνω, which means "to do before." Since it is difficult to decide here regarding the exact meaning of the verb in the context, we have combined two nuances of the verb "to rise early" and "to do the first time" in the translation. The NET Bible considers the expression to mean either to do something the first time ("This is why I originally fled to Tarshish") or to forestall something ("This is what I tried to prevent by fleeing to Tarshish"). The last suggestion, that Jonah wanted to forestall God relenting to bring judgment on Nineveh, makes good sense according to the context here.[7]

8. The second כִּי introduces the object clause of the verb "to know." We may regard the following statement as a compound sentence. The first clause is a noun sentence (one must supply the verb in English), and the second clause uses a participle as the main verb. The second clause with the participle, probably

---

5. Echols, *Reading Jonah*, 72.
6. See Kronholm, "קֶדֶם," 511.
7. *NET Bible*, 1719.

Jonah Complains

indicating frequentative action, enjoys the emphasis. Jonah's real problem—his reason for disobeying God's commission in chapter 1—lies with God relenting concerning bringing calamity on Nineveh. According to Jonah, the cause of his errant behavior does not lie in himself but in God.

9. The characterisation of God in verse 2 occurs throughout Scripture (cf. Exod 34:6; Num 14:18; Neh 9:17, 31; Ps 86:5, 15; 103:8; 145:8; Jer 18:8; Joel 2:13). One cannot fault Jonah on his knowledge of God, yet he still disobeyed God and now he is angry with God.

10. The expression אֶרֶךְ אַפַּיִם literally means "long of nostrils."[8] It is a common Hebrew idiom that means that one does not get angry easily. The origin of the idiom probably stems from equine behavior. A horse expresses anger by breathing roughly through its nostrils; if the nostrils are long, it would take some time for the angry breath to be exhaled. The expression is usually translated as "slow to anger."

11. The term חֶסֶד also deserves an additional comment. As mentioned previously (see comment on Jonah 2:9), it is a key word in the Old Testament and is used to describe the preeminent attribute of "loving-kindness" in God (cf. Ps 136). The translators of the Septuagint coined the word πολυέλεος (lit. "very merciful") to express the meaning of the Hebrew term. Jonah's key problem—as revealed in chapter 1—is that he is not affected by God's חֶסֶד. He has an intellectual understanding of the Lord's attributes, but he has no heart knowledge of the Lord.

12. Verse 2 is one of the most important statements in the book of Jonah; it is a flashback into Jonah's inner thoughts and the reason he disobeyed the Lord's commission in chapter 1. We learn here that Jonah's problem is primarily theological (not personal, political, or racial), not that he does not know God but that he dislikes an aspect of God's character. The prophet

---

8. There is no need to explain the plural אַפַּיִם as a "plural of intensity"; the Hebrew word means "nostril," of which we have two (contra Echols, *Reading Jonah*, 74).

tells us that the reason for his flight before to Tarshish was an act to demonstrate his rebellion against God's command. It appears that he knew that God was omnipresent (cf. Jonah 1:9), but his action, like his behavior in chapter 4, was a means to demonstrate his dissatisfaction with God. Jonah did not like God's propensity to be gracious. Sasson's conclusion is not really correct, "This attitude that extends compassion to all becomes the center of discussion in Jonah 4, since Jonah does not share this view of the narrator or of God."[9] Jonah does share this view of God—we cannot fault Jonah's theology—but he dislikes or does not agree with this attribute of God's nature. It is clear then why Jonah fled to Tarshish and why he was not happy about God preserving Nineveh; it was because he did not want God to be forgiving and compassionate towards them. Why did Jonah not like this aspect of God's nature? The text does not tell us, but we may reflect on Jonah's reasons or logic. Perhaps he saw an inconsistency between God's justice and God's grace, perhaps he thought that God may be more glorified through Nineveh's destruction than through the city's deliverance, or perhaps he thought that people might view God as changing his mind about things and so be regarded as a changeable God. The narrator does not provide the reader with the exact nature of Jonah's dissatisfaction but just points out that Jonah disliked a central aspect of God's nature. This should cause deep introspection in us—whether we may be like Jonah in some ways.

VERSE 3

Hebrew Text and Translation:

וְעַתָּה יְהֹוָה קַח־נָא אֶת־נַפְשִׁי מִמֶּנִּי כִּי טוֹב מוֹתִי מֵחַיָּי: ס

> Therefore now, O LORD, please take my life from me,
> for my death is better than my life."

---

9. Sasson, *Jonah*, 377.

Jonah Complains

Grammatical Analysis:

וְעַתָּה	adverb "now," with conjunction
יְהוָה	proper name, "Yahweh," or conventionally "the LORD"
קַח	Qal, imperative, masculine, singular (לָקַח, to take)
נָא	particle of entreaty
אֶת	direct object marker
נַפְשִׁי	noun, feminine, singular, construct (נֶפֶשׁ, soul, life) with pronominal suffix (first-person, common, singular)
מִמֶּנִּי	preposition מִן, with pronominal suffix (first-person, common, singular)
כִּי	conjunction, "because"
טוֹב	adjective, masculine, singular, absolute (טוֹב, good)
מוֹתִי	noun, masculine, singular, construct (מָוֶת, death), with pronominal suffix (first-person, common, singular)
מֵחַיָּי	noun, masculine, plural, construct (חַי, life), with pronominal suffix (first-person, common, singular), with preposition מִן

Exegetical Notes:

1. After Jonah verbalized his complaint in verse 2, he asked the Lord to take away his life.

2. As a consequence of the complaint stated in verse 2, we may translate the copula *waw* as "therefore."

3. The reason for the request is indicated by the causal clause, introduced with כִּי ("because").

4. Note the syntactical structure expressing comparison (adjective + noun + מִן + noun).

5. Jonah's words are similar to Elijah's (cf. 1 Kgs 19:4). This is another indication of similarity between the book of Jonah

and the story of Elijah. But the irony is that, whereas Elijah endured persecution, Jonah enjoyed success.

VERSE 4

Hebrew Text and Translation:

וַיֹּאמֶר יְהוָה הַהֵיטֵב חָרָה לָךְ:

Then the LORD said, "Is it good for you to be angry?"
(or, Do you have reason to be angry?)

Grammatical Analysis:

וַיֹּאמֶר	Qal, imperfect *waw*-consecutive, third-person, masculine, singular (אָמַר, to say)
יְהוָה	proper name, "Yahweh," or conventionally "the LORD"
הַהֵיטֵב	Hifil, infinitive, absolute (יָטַב, to be good, well), with interrogative הַ
חָרָה	Qal, perfect, third-person, masculine, singular (חָרָה, to burn, be angry)
לָךְ	preposition לְ, with pronominal suffix (second-person, masculine, singular)

Exegetical Notes:

1. Note the use of the interrogative ה before the verb.
2. Note the use of the Hifil infinitive הֵיטֵב (from יָטַב, meaning "to be good"). Literally, "Is it good for you to cause anger."
3. In the Bible, God often confronts the rebellious with questions (cf. Gen 3:9–11; 4:9; 32:27; 1 Kgs 19:9; Job 38:4). God is omniscient and knows the answer to his questions, but he

Jonah Complains

lovingly directs questions to the rebellious to compel them to reflect rationally on their problems and to acknowledge their sin and so lead them to repentance and reconciliation.

VERSE 5

Hebrew Text and Translation:

וַיֵּצֵא יוֹנָה֙ מִן־הָעִ֔יר וַיֵּ֖שֶׁב מִקֶּ֣דֶם לָעִ֑יר וַיַּעַשׂ֩ ל֨וֹ שָׁ֜ם סֻכָּ֗ה וַיֵּ֤שֶׁב תַּחְתֶּ֙יהָ֙ בַּצֵּ֔ל עַ֚ד אֲשֶׁ֣ר יִרְאֶ֔ה מַה־יִּהְיֶ֖ה בָּעִֽיר׃

Then Jonah went out of the city and sat at the east of it. There he made a shelter for himself and sat under it in the shade until he could see what would happen in the city.

Grammatical Analysis:

וַיֵּצֵא	Qal, imperfect *waw*-consecutive, third-person, masculine, singular (יָצָא, to go out)
יוֹנָה	proper name, "Jonah" (alternative meaning, "dove")
מִן	preposition
הָעִיר	noun, feminine, singular, absolute (עִיר, city), with definite article
וַיֵּשֶׁב	Qal, imperfect *waw*-consecutive, third-person, masculine, singular (יָשַׁב, to sit, dwell, remain)
מִקֶּדֶם	noun, masculine, singular, absolute (קֶדֶם, east), with the preposition מִן
לָעִיר	noun, feminine, singular, absolute (עִיר, city), with definite article, and with the preposition לְ
וַיַּעַשׂ	Qal, imperfect *waw*-consecutive, third-person, masculine, singular (עָשָׂה, to do, make)
לוֹ	preposition לְ, with pronominal suffix (third-person, masculine, singular)

127

The Book of Jonah

שָׁם	adverb, "there"
סֻכָּה	noun, feminine, singular, absolute (סֻכָּה, booth, thicket)
וַיֵּשֶׁב	Qal, imperfect *waw*-consecutive, third-person, masculine, singular (יָשַׁב, to sit, dwell, remain)
תַּחְתֶּיהָ	noun, masculine, plural, construct (תַּחַת, the under part, prep. under), with pronominal suffix (third-person, feminine, singular)
בַּצֵּל	noun, masculine, singular, absolute (צֵל, shadow, shade), with preposition בְּ, and the definite article
עַד	preposition, "until"
אֲשֶׁר	relative pronoun
יִרְאֶה	Qal, imperfect, third-person, masculine, singular (רָאָה, to see)
מַה	adverb, "what"
יִהְיֶה	Qal, imperfect, third-person, masculine, singular (הָיָה, to be, become, is)
בָּעִיר	noun, feminine, singular, absolute (עִיר, city), with preposition בְּ, and the definite article

Exegetical Notes:

1. It is interesting to note that Jonah does not respond to the Lord's question.[10] His behavior indicates that he expects the Lord to agree with his wishes and destroy the city. Ironically, before it seemed that Jonah was not happy that God might appear to be changeable, but now Jonah wants God to change his mind!

2. Jonah wants to control God, and through his behavior dictate what God must do. He wants to force God's hand as it were with his recalcitrance.

---

10. A strategy that unbelievers and detractors often use when they are confronted with the facts is silence (cf. Ps 58:1; Mark 3:4).

Jonah Complains

3. Note the use of the preposition מִן־ in the expression מִקֶּדֶם.

VERSE 6

Hebrew Text and Translation:

וַיְמַן יְהוָה־אֱלֹהִים קִיקָיוֹן וַיַּעַל ׀ מֵעַל לְיוֹנָה לִהְיוֹת צֵל עַל־רֹאשׁוֹ לְהַצִּיל לוֹ מֵרָעָתוֹ וַיִּשְׂמַח יוֹנָה עַל־הַקִּיקָיוֹן שִׂמְחָה גְדוֹלָה׃

Then the LORD God appointed a plant, and it grew up over Jonah to be a shade over his head to relieve him from his discomfort. And Jonah was extremely happy about the plant.

Grammatical Analysis:

וַיְמַן	Piel, imperfect *waw*-consecutive, third-person, masculine, singular (מָנָה, to appoint, assign)
יְהוָה	proper name, "Yahweh," or conventionally "the LORD"
אֱלֹהִים	noun, masculine, plural, absolute (אֵל, God)
קִיקָיוֹן	noun, masculine, singular, absolute (קִיקָיוֹן, plant, gourd)
וַיַּעַל	Hifil, imperfect *waw*-consecutive, third-person, masculine, singular (עָלָה, to go up, ascend)
מֵעַל	preposition, with preposition מִן
לְיוֹנָה	proper name, "Jonah" (alternative meaning, "dove"), with the preposition לְ
לִהְיוֹת	Qal, infinitive, construct (הָיָה, to be, become, is), with the preposition לְ
צֵל	noun, masculine, singular, absolute (צֵל, shadow)
עַל	preposition, with pronominal suffix

The Book of Jonah

רֹאשׁוֹ	noun, masculine, singular, construct (רֹאשׁ, head), with pronominal suffix (third-person, masculine, singular)
לְהַצִּיל	Hifil, infinitive, construct (נָצַל, to deliver)
לוֹ	preposition לְ, with pronominal suffix (third-person, masculine, singular)
מֵרָעָתוֹ	noun, feminine, singular, construct (רָעָה, distress, misery, evil), with pronominal suffix (third-person, masculine, singular)
וַיִּשְׂמַח	Qal, imperfect *waw*-consecutive, third-person, masculine, singular (שָׂמַח, to rejoice, be glad)
יוֹנָה	proper name, "Jonah" (alternative meaning, "dove")
עַל	preposition, "on account of" or "about"
הַקִּיקָיוֹן	noun, masculine, singular, absolute (קִיקָיוֹן, plant, gourd), with the definite article
שִׂמְחָה	noun, feminine, singular, construct (שִׂמְחָה, joy, gladness)
גְדוֹלָה	adjective, feminine, singular, absolute (גָדוֹל, great)

Exegetical Notes:

1. Again, we note that the Lord is the main actor in the story. The Lord, in the same way he appointed a fish, now appoints (מָנָה) a plant. We note that there is a literary parallel or correspondence between chapters 2 and 4. In chapter 2 God appointed a fish to save Jonah; now he appoints a gourd and soon a worm to teach Jonah. Such verbal links argue that chapter 2 forms an integrated whole with the rest of the story.

2. Since the exact identity of the plant (קִיקָיוֹן) described here is unknown, most translations render it simply as "plant" (e.g., NKJV, NASB, ESV). In the history of interpretation קִיקָיוֹן is usually understood as a castor oil tree. It is found throughout

Jonah Complains

the Middle East and Mesopotamia. It is a fast-growing shrub with broad leaves that can easily grow up to three meters tall.

3. Note the cognate accusative שִׂמְחָה גְדוֹלָה. Jonah's happiness in verse 6 contrasts with his extreme anger in verse 1.

4. Note that לֹ *lamedh* in לוֹ is used to introduce the direct object of the verb (נָצַל, to deliver). Some scholars have suggested that we may have an indication of dittography here.[11]

VERSE 7

Hebrew Text and Translation:

וַיְמַן הָאֱלֹהִים תּוֹלַעַת בַּעֲלוֹת הַשַּׁחַר לַמָּחֳרָת
וַתַּךְ אֶת־הַקִּיקָיוֹן וַיִּיבָשׁ׃

But then God appointed a worm. And when dawn came the next day, it attacked the plant and it withered.

Grammatical Analysis:

וַיְמַן	Piel, imperfect *waw*-consecutive, third-person, masculine, singular (מָנָה, to appoint, assign)
הָאֱלֹהִים	noun, masculine, plural, absolute (אֵל, God), with the definite article
תּוֹלַעַת	noun, feminine, singular, absolute (תּוֹלֵעָה, worm)
בַּעֲלוֹת	Qal, infinitive, construct (עָלָה, to go up, ascend), with preposition בְּ
הַשַּׁחַר	noun, masculine, singular, absolute (שַׁחַר, dawn), with the definite article
לַמָּחֳרָת	noun, feminine, singular, absolute (מָחֳרָת, the morrow), with the preposition לְ

11. Dittography refers to the scribal error when a copyist unintentionally repeats letters or words when copying a manuscript.

וַתַּ֛ךְ	Hifil, imperfect *waw*-consecutive, third-person, feminine, singular (נָכָה, to smite)
אֶת	direct object marker
הַקִּיקָי֖וֹן	noun, masculine, singular, absolute (קִיקָיוֹן, plant, gourd), with the definite article
וַיִּיבָֽשׁ	Qal, imperfect *waw*-consecutive, third-person, masculine, singular (יָבֵשׁ, to be dry, wither)

Exegetical Notes:

1. After the plant provided shade to Jonah, God appointed a worm, and it ruined the plant. Note the change from the LORD (יְהוָה) to God (הָאֱלֹהִים). The word "God" (אֱלֹהִים) occurs sixteen times in the book of Jonah.[12] Apart from Jonah 1:5, it always refers to the God of Israel. On five occasions the term is used with the article (Jonah 1:6; 3:9, 10; 4:7).

2. The worm (תּוֹלַעַת) is sometimes used in the Bible as a symbol of insignificance (e.g., Job 25:6; Ps 22:7; Isa 41:14).

3. The expression בַּעֲלוֹת הַשַּׁחַר literally means "in the going up (Qal, infinitive, construct) of the dawn."

4. The verb יָבֵשׁ ("to be dry," "to wither") is used in the context of the Exodus when the Lord dried up the rivers of the Jordan so that the Israelites could enter the promised land (Josh 2:10; 4:23; cf. Isa 42:15; 44:27; Jer 51:36). The verb is also used in connection with judgment (e.g., Ezek 17:24; 19:12).

VERSE 8

Hebrew Text and Translation:

וַיְהִ֣י׀ כִּזְרֹ֣חַ הַשֶּׁ֗מֶשׁ וַיְמַ֨ן אֱלֹהִ֜ים ר֤וּחַ קָדִים֙ חֲרִישִׁ֔ית

---

12. See Jonah 1:5, 6, 9; 2:1, 6; 3:3, 5, 8, 9, 10; 4:2, 6, 7, 8, 9. In Jonah 4:2 the term אֵל (singular) is used.

Jonah Complains

וַיְהִ֣י ׀ כִּזְרֹ֣חַ הַשֶּׁ֗מֶשׁ וַיְמַ֨ן אֱלֹהִ֜ים ר֤וּחַ קָדִים֙ חֲרִישִׁ֔ית וַתַּ֥ךְ הַשֶּׁ֛מֶשׁ עַל־רֹ֥אשׁ יוֹנָ֖ה וַיִּתְעַלָּ֑ף וַיִּשְׁאַ֤ל אֶת־נַפְשׁוֹ֙ לָמ֔וּת וַיֹּ֕אמֶר ט֥וֹב מוֹתִ֖י מֵחַיָּֽי:

When the sun came up, God appointed a sultry east wind, and the sun beat down on Jonah's head so that he became faint and pleaded with all his soul to die. And he said, "My death is better than my life."

Grammatical Analysis:

וַיְהִי	Qal, imperfect *waw*-consecutive, third-person, masculine, singular (הָיָה, to be, become, is)
כִּזְרֹחַ	Qal, infinitive, construct (זָרַח, to rise, come forth), with preposition כְּ
הַשֶּׁמֶשׁ	noun, feminine, singular, absolute (שֶׁמֶשׁ, sun), with the definite article
וַיְמַן	Piel, imperfect *waw*-consecutive, third-person, masculine, singular (מָנָה, to appoint, assign)
אֱלֹהִים	noun, masculine, plural, absolute (אֵל, God)
רוּחַ	noun, feminine, singular, construct (רוּחַ, wind)
קָדִים	noun, masculine, singular, absolute (קָדִים, east, east wind)
חֲרִישִׁית	adjective, feminine, absolute (חֲרִישִׁי, hot, sultry)
וַתַּךְ	Hifil, imperfect *waw*-consecutive, third-person, feminine, singular (נָכָה, to smite)
הַשֶּׁמֶשׁ	noun, feminine, singular, absolute (שֶׁמֶשׁ, sun), with the definite article
עַל	preposition, "on" or "upon"
רֹאשׁ	noun, masculine, singular, construct (רֹאשׁ, head)
יוֹנָה	proper name, "Jonah" (alternative meaning, "dove")

The Book of Jonah

וַיִּתְעַלָּף	Hithpael, imperfect *waw*-consecutive, third-person, masculine, singular (עָלַף, to enwrap oneself, swoon away)
וַיִּשְׁאַל	Qal, imperfect *waw*-consecutive, third-person, masculine, singular (שָׁאַל, to ask, inquire)
אֶת	preposition, "with"
נַפְשׁוֹ	noun, feminine, singular, absolute (נֶפֶשׁ, soul, life) with pronominal suffix (third-person, masculine, singular)
לָמוּת	Qal, infinitive, construct (מוּת, to die), with preposition לְ
וַיֹּאמֶר	Qal, imperfect *waw*-consecutive, third-person, masculine, singular (אָמַר, to say)
טוֹב	adjective, masculine, singular, absolute (טוֹב, good)
מוֹתִי	noun, masculine, singular, construct (מָוֶת, death), with pronominal suffix (first-person, common, singular)
מֵחַיָּי	noun, masculine, plural, construct (חַי, life), with pronominal suffix (first-person, common, singular), with preposition מִן

Exegetical Notes:

1. Note the use of the infinitive construct with the preposition to introduce an adverbial clause of time, כִּזְרֹחַ הַשֶּׁמֶשׁ ("when the sun came up").

2. Without the shade the plant provided, the heat of the sun exasperated Jonah.

3. The term חֲרִישִׁית occurs only once in the Bible. A term occurring only once is referred to as a *hapax legomenon* (lit. "once said"); the plural expression is *hapax legomena*. Since interpreters do not have other examples of the use of such words in the Bible, it is often difficult to ascertain their meaning. The meaning of חֲרִישִׁית is proposed to be "sultry,"

Jonah Complains

"scorching," or "hot." The Septuagint has συγκαίοντι (present, participle, active, from συγκαίω, "to burn").

4. Note the use of the Hithpael וַיִּתְעַלָּף, which conveys the meaning that Jonah fainted within himself. There was nothing within himself to sustain him any longer. Both physically and spiritually Jonah ran out of energy.

5. Among other things, the episode of Jonah and the gourd shows that all of life is governed and sustained by the merciful hand of God.

6. Here אֶת is the preposition "with." The expression אֶת־נַפְשׁוֹ means "with his soul." Since the term is also used to express strong desire or emotion, we follow the NASB rendering "with all his soul," i.e., "earnestly."[13] The wording of the ESV does not translate the prepositional phrase. The ASV has "requested for himself." It seems that Jonah no longer prays to God, he murmurs only to himself. His spiritual situation now appears to be worse than when he was in the belly of the fish.

VERSE 9

Hebrew Text and Translation:

וַיֹּאמֶר אֱלֹהִים אֶל־יוֹנָה הַהֵיטֵב חָרָה־לְךָ עַל־הַקִּיקָיוֹן
וַיֹּאמֶר הֵיטֵב חָרָה־לִי עַד־מָוֶת׃

Then God said to Jonah, "Is it good for you to be angry about the plant? (Do you have good reason to be angry about the plant?)" And he said, "It is good for me to be angry, even to death (I have good reason to be angry, even to death)."

---

13. The LXX here translates the Hebrew as, καὶ ἀπελέγετο τὴν ψυχὴν αὐτοῦ, "and he gave up his soul . . ."

The Book of Jonah

Grammatical Analysis:

וַיֹּאמֶר	Qal, imperfect *waw*-consecutive, third-person, masculine, singular (אָמַר, to say)
אֱלֹהִים	noun, masculine, plural, absolute (אֵל, God)
אֶל	preposition
יוֹנָה	proper name, "Jonah" (alternative meaning, "dove")
הַהֵיטֵב	Hifil, infinitive, absolute (יָטַב, to be good, well), with interrogative הֲ
חָרָה	Qal, perfect, third-person, person, masculine, singular (חָרָה, to burn, be angry)
לְךָ	preposition, with pronominal suffix (second-person, masculine, singular)
עַל	preposition
הַקִּיקָיוֹן	noun, masculine, singular, absolute (קִיקָיוֹן, plant, gourd), with definite article
וַיֹּאמֶר	Qal, imperfect *waw*-consecutive, third-person, masculine, singular (אָמַר, to say)
הֵיטֵב	Hifil, infinitive, absolute (יָטַב, to be good, well)
חָרָה	Qal, perfect, third-person, masculine, singular (חָרָה, to burn, be angry)
לִי	preposition, with pronominal suffix (first-person, common, singular)
עַד	preposition
מָוֶת	noun, masculine, singular, absolute (מָוֶת, death)

Exegetical Notes:

1. Note again the use of interrogative הֲ, transforming the statement into a question.

Jonah Complains

2. Apart from the prepositional phrase עַל־הַקִּיקָיוֹן, the wording of the question is the same as in verse 4. Whereas before Jonah did not bother to answer the question, this time he is even angrier and answers defiantly, "It is good for me to be angry, even to death."

3. This episode of Jonah's extreme dissatisfaction with his physical circumstances reveals the fickleness of human nature. Jonah's complaint has become totally irrational and petty. Before in chapter 1, Jonah was a bastion of strength and self-sacrifice. He did not fear anything and was prepared to die for others. At the beginning of chapter 4 he revealed himself to act out of great theological principles and implied that God's nature is problematic. However, having been exposed to the elements for a little while, he now behaved like an immature toddler. What happened to his great courage and deep theological principles (cf. Eccl 1:8; Isa 40:6–8; Jer 17:9; Eph 4:14; Jas 1:8)?

4. Even after his experience of chapter 2, Jonah is not a totally changed man. There was regret in chapter 2 but no real and lasting repentance (see comments on Jonah 2:10 in note 8). Regret and obedience are not enough; the people of God also need to know God intimately and then be transformed by that knowledge to reflect God's mercy and love.

VERSE 10

Hebrew Text and Translation:

וַיֹּאמֶר יְהוָה אַתָּה חַסְתָּ עַל־הַקִּיקָיוֹן אֲשֶׁר לֹא־עָמַלְתָּ בּוֹ
וְלֹא גִדַּלְתּוֹ שֶׁבִּן־לַיְלָה הָיָה וּבִן־לַיְלָה אָבָד:

> Then the LORD said, "You (yourself) pitied the plant for which you had not worked and which you had not caused to grow, which came up overnight and perished overnight (lit. "which overnight was (son of the night) and which overnight (son of a night) perished),

The Book of Jonah

Grammatical Analysis:

וַיֹּאמֶר	Qal, imperfect *waw*-consecutive, third-person, masculine, singular (אָמַר, to say)
יְהוָה	proper name, "Yahweh," or conventionally "the LORD"
אַתָּה	second personal pronoun, singular
חַסְתָּ	Qal, perfect, second-person, masculine, singular (חוּס, to pity, have compassion)
עַל	preposition
הַקִּיקָיוֹן	noun, masculine, singular, absolute (קִיקָיוֹן, plant, gourd), with definite article
אֲשֶׁר	relative pronoun
לֹא	adverb "not"
עָמַלְתָּ	Qal, perfect, second-person, masculine, singular (עָמַל, to labour, toil)
בּוֹ	preposition, with pronominal suffix (third-person, masculine, singular)
וְלֹא	adverb "not," with conjunction וְ
גִדַּלְתּוֹ	Piel, perfect, second-person, masculine, singular (גָּדַל, to grow up, become great)
שֶׁבִּן	noun, masculine, singular, construct (בֵּן, son), with relative pronoun שֶׁ
לַיְלָה	noun, masculine, singular, absolute (לַיְלָה, night)
הָיָה	Qal, perfect, third-person, masculine, singular (הָיָה, to be, is)
וּבִן	noun, masculine, singular, construct (בֵּן, son), with conjunction
לַיְלָה	noun, masculine, singular, absolute (לַיְלָה, night)
אָבָד	Qal, perfect, third-person, masculine, singular (אָבַד, to perish)

Jonah Complains

Exegetical Notes:

1. The Lord has the last word in the book of Jonah. The word of the Lord commences the book; so too the word of the Lord concludes the narrative.

2. It is interesting to note that there are thirty-nine words in the last direct quotation. Jonah's complaint at the beginning of the chapter also contains thirty-nine words (verses 2 to 3).

3. Observe that the Lord's question to Jonah begins with the personal pronoun "you" (אַתָּה). It is placed at the beginning of the sentence for emphasis. Since the pronoun is already contained in the Hebrew verb form (חַסְתָּ) we may add the reflexive "yourself" in the English translation to bring out the emphasis.

4. Note the perfect tense of the verb חַסְתָּ (from חוּס, "to pity," "to have compassion," "to be concerned about") describing past action. The Bible uses the same verb to describe the pity God took on the Israelites (Ezek 16:5; in Ps 72:13 the LORD's pity towards the gentiles is celebrated).

5. Note the perfect tenses of עָמַלְתָּ and גִדַּלְתּוֹ, which we should translate with the pluperfect in English since they indicate action (or non-action!) prior to the action of the previous verb.

6. The idiomatic expression שֶׁבִּן־לַיְלָה הָיָה וּבִן־לַיְלָה אָבָד describes the transitory nature of the plant. Note the particle שֶׁ which is an abbreviation of the relative pronoun אֲשֶׁר.

VERSE 11

Hebrew Text and Translation:

וַאֲנִי לֹא אָחוּס עַל־נִינְוֵה הָעִיר הַגְּדוֹלָה
אֲשֶׁר יֶשׁ־בָּהּ הַרְבֵּה מִשְׁתֵּים־עֶשְׂרֵה רִבּוֹ אָדָם
אֲשֶׁר לֹא־יָדַע בֵּין־יְמִינוֹ לִשְׂמֹאלוֹ וּבְהֵמָה רַבָּה׃

but should I (Myself) not have pity on Nineveh, the great city, in which there are more than 120,000 people who

The Book of Jonah

do not know the difference between their right and left hand, as well as much livestock?"

Grammatical Analysis:

וַאֲנִי	first personal pronoun, singular, with the conjunction
לֹא	adverb "not"
אָחוּס	Qal, perfect, first-person, common, singular (חוּס, to pity, have compassion)
עַל	preposition
נִינְוֵה	proper noun, "Nineveh"
הָעִיר	noun, feminine, singular, absolute (עִיר, city), with definite article
הַגְּדוֹלָה	adjective, feminine, singular, absolute (גָּדוֹל, great), with definite article
אֲשֶׁר	relative pronoun
יֶשׁ	particle of existence, "there is"
בָּהּ	preposition, with pronominal suffix (third-person, feminine, singular)
הַרְבֵּה	Hifil, infinitive, absolute (רָבָה, to be great, much, many)
מִשְׁתֵּים	noun, feminine, dual, construct (שְׁנַיִם, two), with preposition מִן
עֶשְׂרֵה	noun, common, singular, absolute (עָשָׂר, ten)
רִבּוֹ	noun, common, singular, absolute (רִבּוֹ, ten thousand, myriad)
אָדָם	noun, masculine, plural, construct (אָדָם, man, mankind)
אֲשֶׁר	relative pronoun
לֹא	adverb "not"

Jonah Complains

יָדַע	Qal, perfect, third-person, masculine, singular (יָדַע, to know)
בֵּין	preposition "between"
יְמִינוֹ	noun, feminine, singular, absolute (יָמִין, right hand), with pronominal suffix (third-person, masculine, singular)
לִשְׂמֹאלוֹ	noun, common, singular, absolute (שְׂמֹאול, left hand), with pronominal suffix (third-person, masculine, singular), with preposition לְ
וּבְהֵמָה	noun, feminine, singular, absolute (בְּהֵמָה, animal, cattle, livestock), with conjunction
רַבָּה	adjective, feminine, singular, absolute (רַב, much, many, great)

Exegetical Notes:

1. From the context we may discern that the last statement in the book of Jonah is a question (וַאֲנִי לֹא אָחוּס).[14]

2. The conjunction *waw* implies a comparison or a contrast between Jonah and the Lord, so we have translated it as "but."

3. As before, the personal pronoun אֲנִי stands before the verb for emphasis. Since the pronoun is already contained in the Hebrew verb form (אָחוּס), we may add the reflexive "myself" in the English translation to bring out the emphasis.

4. The NET Bible provides further explanation regarding the different nuances of the verb חוּס (to pity, have compassion). It "has a basic threefold range of meanings: 1) 'to be troubled about'; 2) 'to look with compassion upon'; and 3) 'to show pity, to spare,' with respect to death/judgment. In v. 10 it refers to Jonah's lament over the death of his plant, meaning 'to

---

14. Note Echols: "The context of the verse indicates that it is a question, but the normal interrogatives are missing." See Echols, *Reading Jonah*, 86.

be upset about' or 'to be troubled about'. However, here in v. 11 it means, regarding judgment, 'to show pity, spare.'"[15]

5. The expression הָעִיר הַגְּדוֹלָה stands in apposition to the proper name Nineveh.

6. Note the use of הַרְבֵּה (Hifil, infinitive, absolute; from רָבָה, "be many," "be great," "to increase").

7. Note that the preposition מִן may express comparison: "more than."

8. The term רִבּוֹ is a numeral, meaning "ten thousand." According to Echols, it "may be an Aramaic loanword."[16]

9. The singular אָדָם is used collectively for "people."

10. The expression לֹא־יָדַע בֵּין־יְמִינוֹ לִשְׂמֹאלוֹ ("who do not know the difference between their right and left hand") has moral overtones. The author depicts the Ninevites as being morally naïve. In other words, their wickedness was done in ignorance. Their eagerness to repent illustrates that they did not sin willfully.

11. Note the use of the perfect tense יָדַע. In Hebrew, the perfect may be used to express characteristic patterns (general truths or maxims), the so called "characteristic perfect."

12. The book of Jonah famously ends with the memorable expression וּבְהֵמָה רַבָּה ("and much livestock"). God is not only concerned for people but also for animals (cf. Deut 25:4; Ps 36:6; Prov 12:10; Matt 6:26; 10:29).

13. Although the narrator does not record Jonah's answer, the final statement is not a rhetorical question. It is a real question which immediately extracts an answer—whether mentally or verbally—from the readers or hearers of the story. The logic of the question is irrefutable. Certainly, the lives of 120,000 Ninevites and numerous livestock are much more precious than a transitory plant. Those who do not answer in

---

15. *NET Bible*, 1721.
16. Echols, *Reading Jonah*, 87.

Jonah Complains

the affirmative (i.e., God should not pity) reveal themselves not only to be irrational but also callous. Those who answer in the affirmative (i.e., God should pity) acknowledge God's sovereign grace in his disposal of forgiveness and salvation.

14. But the purpose of the book of Jonah is much more than mere verbal assent or intellectual understanding: the book teaches that for God's people to be God's witnesses in the world—to become effective servants of the Lord—there also needs to be a transformation of the heart. The goal of the Christian life is not only to know God but to imitate God and the Lord Jesus.[17]

15. Note the concluding remark in Nogalski's commentary: "We are not called to be the distributors of divine justice, but we are called the vehicle of grace."[18] The servant of the Lord will be an able and willing servant only when he or she is affected by the Lord's grace in the history of salvation which has found its fulfillment and most remarkable illustration in the sign of Jonah—the amazing love of God which stands behind the death and resurrection of the Lord Jesus (Matt 12:39; 2 Cor 5:14; 1 John 4:10).

---

17. Timmer, *Gracious and Compassionate God*, 146–54.
18. Nogalski, *Books of Joel, Obadiah, and Jonah*, 396.

Selected Bibliography

Barker, Kenneth L., ed. *The NIV Study Bible.* Grand Rapids: Zondervan, 1985.
Brown, A. Philip, and Bryan W. Smith. *A Reader's Hebrew Bible.* Grand Rapids: Zondervan, 2008.
Brown, F., Driver, S. R., and Briggs, C. A., eds. *A Hebrew and English Lexicon of the Old Testament.* Oxford: Clarendon, 1952.
Calvin, John. *John Calvin Bible Commentaries: The Books of Jonah, Micah, Nahum.* Translated by John King. Altenmünster: Jazzybee Verlag, 2017.
Cathcart, Kevin J., and Gordon, Robert P. *The Targum of the Minor Prophets.* The Aramaic Bible 14. Edinburgh: T. & T. Clark, 1989.
Chisholm, Robert B. *A Workbook for Intermediate Hebrew: Grammar, Exegesis, and Commentary on Jonah and Ruth.* Grand Rapids: Kregel, 2006.
Clark, David J., et al. *A Handbook on the Books of Obadiah, Jonah, and Micah.* USA: United Bible Societies, 1993.
Davidson, Benjamin. *The Analytical Hebrew and Chaldee Lexicon.* Grand Rapids: Zondervan, 1970.
Day, John. *From Creation to Babel: Studies in Genesis 1–11.* New York: Bloomsbury, 2013.
Echols, Charles L. *Reading Jonah: A Guide to the Hebrew Text.* Charles L. Echols, 2013.
Ferreira, Johan. *Old Testament Hebrew: Essential Vocabulary, Grammar and Syntax for Exegesis.* Toowong, Australia: Bible College of Queensland, 2008.
Ferreira, Johan. "A Note on Jonah 2.8: Idolatry and Inhumanity in Israel." *The Bible Translator* 63 (2012) 28–38.
Harris, Robert L., Gleason L. Archer, and Bruce K. Waltke, eds. *Theological Wordbook of the Old Testament.* 2 vols. Chicago: Moody, 1980.
Jenson, Philip. *Reading Jonah.* Grove Biblical Series 14. Cambridge: Grove, 1999.
Jepsen, A. "אָמַן." In *Theological Dictionary of the Old Testament, Vol. 1*, edited by G. Johannes Botterweck and Helmer Ringgren, 308. Translated by John T. Willis. Grand Rapids: Eerdmans, 1977.
Kahle, Paul. *The Cairo Geniza.* Oxford: Blackwell, 1959.

Selected Bibliography

Keil, Carl Friedrich. *The Twelve Minor Prophets.* Edinburgh: T. & T. Clark, 1871.
Kittel, Rudolf, ed. *Biblia Hebraica Stuttgartensia.* Stuttgart: Deutsche Bibelgesellschaft, 1997.
Kronholm, T. "קָדַם." In *Theological Dictionary of the Old Testament, vol. 12*, edited by G. Johannes Botterweck, Helmer Ringgren, and Heinz-Josef Fabry, 511. Translated by Douglas W. Stott. Grand Rapids: Eerdmans, 2003.
Kugel, James L. *The Idea of Biblical Poetry: Parallelism and Its History.* New Haven: Yale University Press, 1981.
Limburg, James. *Jonah: A Commentary.* Louisville: Westminster/John Knox, 1993.
Lowth, Robert. *Lectures on the Sacred Poetry of the Hebrews.* London: S. Chadwick & Co., 1847.
Manley, George Thomas, Godfrey C. Robinson, and Alan M. Stibbs, eds. *The New Bible Handbook.* London: IVP, 1965.
Martin, Hugh. *A Commentary on Jonah.* Carlisle, PA: Banner of Truth Trust, 1982.
Moberly, R. W. L. "אמן." In *New International Dictionary of Old Testament Theology and Exegesis, Vol 1.*, edited by Willem A. VanGemeren, 432. Grand Rapids: Zondervan, 1997.
NET Bible, Full Notes Edition. 2nd ed. Nashville: Thomas Nelson, 2019.
Nogalski, James D., and Marvin A. Sweeney, eds. *Reading and Hearing the Book of the Twelve.* Atlanta: SBL, 2000.
Nogalski, James D. *The Books of Joel, Obadiah, and Jonah.* New International Commentary on the Old Testament. Grand Rapids: Eerdmans, 2023.
Patterson, Richard D., and Andrew E. Hill. *Cornerstone Biblical Commentary, Vol. 10: Minor Prophets, Hosea–Malachi.* Carol Stream, IL: Tyndale House, 2008.
Perowne, Thomas Thomason. *Obadiah and Jonah, with Notes and Introduction.* Cambridge: Cambridge University Press, 1889.
Petersen, David L., and Kent Harold Richards. *Interpreting Hebrew Poetry.* Minneapolis: Augsburg Fortress, 1992.
Petit, Lucas P., and D. Morandi Bonacossi. *Nineveh, the Great City: Symbol of Beauty and Power.* PALMA 13. Leiden: Sidestone, 2017.
Sakenfeld, Katharine Doob. *The Meaning of Hesed in the Hebrew Bible: A New Inquiry.* HSM 17. Missoula, MT: Scholars, 1978.
Sasson, Jack M. *Jonah: A New Translation with Introduction, Commentary, and Interpretation.* The Anchor Bible 24B. New York: Doubleday, 1990.
Sheck, Thomas P., ed. *Commentaries on the Twelve Prophets: Vol. 1, Ancient Christian Texts by Jerome.* Downers Grove, IL: IVP Academic, 2016.
Snaith, Norman Henry. *Notes on the Hebrew Text of Jonah.* London: Epworth, 1945.
Sproul, R. C., ed. *The Reformation Study Bible: English Standard Version.* Orlando: Reformation Trust, 2015.

Selected Bibliography

Timmer, Daniel C. *A Gracious and Compassionate God: Mission, Salvation and Spirituality in the Book of Jonah.* Downers Grove, IL: InterVarsity, 2011.

Tov, Emanuel. "The Textual Value of the Septuagint Version of the Minor Prophets." In *Les Douze Prophètes dans la LXX: Protocoles et procédures dans la traduction grecque: stylistique, poétique et histoire,* edited by Cécile Dogniez and Philippe le Moigne, VTSup 180, 129–48. Leiden: Brill, 2019.

Trible, Phyllis. *Studies in the Book of Jonah.* PhD dissertation, Columbia University, 1963.

Trible, Phyllis. *Rhetorical Criticism: Context, Method, and the Book of Jonah.* Philadelphia: Fortress, 1994.

Vos, Geerhardus. *Biblical Theology: Old and New Testaments.* Grand Rapids: Eerdmans, 1980.

Watson, Wilfred G. E. *Classical Hebrew Poetry: A Guide to Its Techniques.* 2nd ed. Sheffield: Sheffield Academic Press, 1989.

Wiseman, Donald J., David W. Baker, T. Desmond Alexander, and Bruce K. Waltke. *Obadiah, Jonah and Micah: An Introduction and Commentary 26.* Downers Grove, IL: InterVarsity, 1988.

Wolff, Hans Walter. *Obadiah and Jonah: A Commentary.* Translated by Margaret Kohl. Minneapolis: Augsburg, 1986.

www.ingramcontent.com/pod-product-compliance
Lightning Source LLC
Chambersburg PA
CBHW072144160426
43197CB00012B/2238